MAY 1 3 2020

REMOVED
from Collection

D1090779

Louisburg Library
Bringing People and Information Together

Resilient Walker

A Memoir

Dr. Shree Walker

Library District No. 1
Louisburg Library
206 S. Broadway
Louisburg, KS 66053

Copyright © 2018 by Shree Walker.

All rights reserved. No portion of this book may be reproduced in any form without permission from the publisher, except as permitted by U.S. copyright law.

For permissions contact: Shree.Walker@ResilientWalker.com.

This is a working memoir. In most instances, the information presented is largely subject to the author's memory and perspective. I have attempted to research verifiable facts; however, many instances will be delivered the way I remember them. Names have been changed in certain instances, but the truth, as I remember it, has remained the same and been borne out.

All Scripture quotations are from *The Holy Bible, English Standard Version*. ESV® Text Edition: 2016.

ISBN- 10: 1729515061
ISBN- 13: 9781729515068

For the little girl within, you are now free to heal.

Resilient Walker

Sleep Walker

Sleep

From a mess of sweat-stained sheets, Shree kicked her legs up, swung them out over the bed, and dropped them to the dusty floor, arousing from her sleep. Sleep, that elusive elixir of rest, that promise of new beginnings, that hope for tomorrow—when it's most anticipated—never seems to come. Sleep, that concoction of apathy and hopelessness, chaining prisoners to their own bed like captives of the most satiating drug, is a foreshadowing of death. Sleep. Everyone was *sleep*. Everyone clung to their sheets like June beetles to window screens, still *sleep*. Everyone, except her.

The house sweltered that morning, sweaty and cramped. Frankie, the mother, lay half-strewn across the bed, mostly covered, next to Memphis, her boyfriend, who hogged most of the sheets. Connie, Frankie's son, who was sixteen at best, cuddled up to his girlfriend on a pallet on the floor. His girlfriend was twelve years his senior. More children, four more children slept in one other room, bodies everywhere, ignorant of the pre-dawn life. Everyone was *sleep*, except Shree.

She was walking, not sleepwalking, but walking with purpose. Following the orange extension cord that meandered through the house, across the carpet and over the linoleum, through the crack in the back door, Shree walked—in the dark. She opened the creaking door, held it for just a moment to keep it from slamming, and then slowly removed her hand. The heat rose off the concrete driveway surrounding the generator that idly sat connected to the orange extension cord waiting to provide the only means of electricity on this dry August morning in the southern section of Los Angeles, California. Shree pulled the cord rapidly—three times—the power surged, and the silence broke.

The generator hummed and Shree's morning sprang to life. She grabbed her outfit, one of her three, plugged in the iron, and went to work. Work, meaning making herself better, was what Shree was all about. While the world slept, she found solace in growing, studying, learning. And this morning was no different. Why was Shree up so early taking on the day while those around her slept? Because today was a school day, and to Shree, school was very significant—a link to the future. And the future she wanted for herself was freedom, whatever that meant.

Plugging in the other necessity for her morning routine, the radio cassette tape player, Shree popped in a tape of Luther Vandross. Luther belted out "Always and Forever" in the background and steam rose from the iron as she settled into her morning routine.

But it hadn't always been this way. In fact, it hadn't been this way for very long: this house, this routine, these people. No, it hadn't. Shree currently attended her fourth high school in as many years; her resiliency fading, and although she walked with purpose, her heart melted slowly inside her. Unbeknownst to her, her body settled into its own mourning routine: mourning the loss of childhood, mourning the sexual abuse, mourning the nomadic lifestyle thrust upon her. *Exhausted* didn't describe it; it was more like *broken*—but without realizing it. She barely hung on, yet in her mind this feeling was as normal as crushing crawling cockroaches that escaped from the cabinet.

Which is what she did. Opening the white cabinet door with the bruised corner and flaky paint encouraged the critters to emerge. With one hand, Shree killed the roaches, with the other, she pulled out the sugar-frosted cereal. Although the action was listless, Shree burst with energy. Although her past haunted her, suffocated her like the sleep was suffocating the others in the house, Shree remained encouraged. She didn't see her past chasing her down, emerging in her future. Like a lemming heading toward a cliff, she walked the same path she walked since childhood—determined but detached. The dense fog had not descended upon her, but the symptoms had.

Her grades dropped, but her smile didn't fade. Her love for studying Socrates and Plato, Aristotle and Henry David Thoreau evaporated, but her resiliency didn't. Her automated behaviors of rising early, working hard, and encouraging herself worked, but she pressed against a wall she couldn't see. Maybe she was sleepwalking. If only she knew.

The house was still dark, the generator still buzzing, but Luther Vandross had died off with the last crunch of the cereal. Shree donned her outfit, gathered her notebooks, and opened the front door to face the day. As the sun peeked over the horizon across the flat land in southern California, Shree closed the door. And, yes, everyone was still *sleep.*

Walking. Walking was great. Walking meant progress, and walking meant freedom. Walking gave her time to think and breathe, and just to exist. It wasn't drudgery; it was hopeful, cathartic even. And it was part of her new routine. Shree walked to school. She walked miles to her new high school, Fremont High School. Hope was found there because education was found there. And education was important. Education quieted the voices.

For as long as she could remember, voices had derided her. Often, she heard the dismissive voices of others, but the worst voice was internal. The most haunting voice for Shree was her own. She told herself, *Don't end up on welfare.* Frankie was on welfare. Although Frankie worked, she braided hair and did other odd jobs, Shree's mother had six children, a live-in boyfriend, and a not-too-endearing financial past. *Don't end up on welfare like Momma. Don't have a baby young like Momma.*

A few months prior, she had been scared—it wasn't her fault she was thrust into this life of sexuality—she had thought she might be pregnant. Shree had been sexually abused as a young girl multiple times, inappropriately fondled by a family member in her middle teens, and a few years later, raped. It wasn't her fault, but her voices said, *Don't get pregnant young. You'll never make it.* She had been scared, now she was just scarred.

You have to go to school to be successful. You have to at least graduate. So she prayed and she walked. Praying was new, relatively new. About three years earlier, she had begun praying. Her high school GPA had slipped to a 2.1, so like many high-school students just before the test, she had prayed. Maybe this was the beginning of a new journey—Shree didn't know. Now was a time for survival, and she wore the tread bare on her shoes as she walked to school, praying and dreaming.

Would she make it, or was it all just a dream? Maybe she was sleep-walking. *Why not just sleep like everyone else?* The voices came and went, the apartments and houses came and went, her mother's boy-friends came and went, but the walking remained—and the resiliency. Her life to this point had been nasty, brutish, and short, and it begged two questions. Would she become hard and cracked and flake into dust like the pavement upon which she walked, or would she become . . . a resilient walker?

Resilient Walker

"You are going through it, aren't you?"—Shree Walker

This isn't an unprecedented memoir, not an eye-popping, rags-to-riches story written to leave you breathless and in need of towels to dry the tears. This story is simple, though the journey was perilous, injurious, and full of broken dreams and staunch reality. A story of a little girl growing up to do quite normal things in a normal world. The story is simple, but the struggle was real. The "normal" atrocities of my childhood are all too common, and they block children from ever accomplishing the "normal" successes for many Americans. What many people have accepted as milk and bread to urban life are the poverty and violence that rip the pages out of far too many children's lives. My story is only different because I made it out. My story reveals the awesome power of combining a state of being (resiliency) and a continual action (walking). Most of us have already witnessed this power; therefore, the story isn't new or revolutionary, but it is a reminder—a reminder of what you and I have learned in our past, from our past, and ought to practice today. No, this isn't an unprecedented memoir, it's only a story of a journey back to a human experience we can all understand, back to our true selves, who we were meant to be.

To be resilient is to be one who can persevere through the midst of the storm. Resiliency means to be able to withstand homelessness, abandonment, rape, sexual abuse, a nomadic lifestyle, the loss of family members, survivor's remorse. To be resilient is to be flexible, to be bendable—but unbreakable. To walk is to stay in motion, to proceed through, to press forward, perpetually. Walking is a form of transportation, a means of traveling from place to place, a time to clear your head.

Resiliency alone means you can take anything, but you don't do anything. Walking simply means you keep on walking, you walk over, around, and away from conflict, but you never walk *through* anything. Resiliency is a state of being. Walking is a progressive action. To be a resilient walker is to walk through pain and heartbreak into joy and comfort, to proceed through trials and tears, to stop to smile and play, to withstand torment, to sing loudly, to be present, to show empathy, to withstand the evil in order to do the greater good. To be a resilient walker is to realize that the world is full of monsters with friendly faces and angels full of scars. To be a resilient walker means never to be only resilient or only walking, but to marry the two, so they can hold hands with one who knows the difference.

Voices

A Voice Indeed

"Little children, let us not love in word or talk, but in deed and in truth."–1 John 3:18

On the drive back home, the thoughts finally clicked. Long after the seatbelt engaged the buckle, my mind grasped the elusive thoughts it had been reaching for earlier in the evening. The glare of the passing headlights was mildly blinding, but the illumination I realized was reflected in those lights. Although painful, my past experiences brought me to a place where I could be a beacon for others. I felt a kinship to the subjects in Plato's *Allegory of the Cave*—the enlightenment hurt, but with it came freedom. *I wasn't just a voice*—though I indeed have a voice—*I was a voice, indeed.*

Let me back up a moment. Don't forgive me for my scattered thoughts because I'm not asking. I have already been forgiven. I'm asking you to hang with me while I unwind this tale that I fully began to understand a few months ago at a barbeque joint—of all places. I was sitting right smack dab in the middle, exposed, when he asked me . . . The thick, resonant smell of hickory smoke and roasted ribs floated through the lacquered-wood dining area and collided with his question. Had I not been prepared, it may have been overwhelming. But my life had prepared me—as a pain surrogate—to tackle tough questions with finesse and fervor. He, the interviewer, looked me dead in the eye and asked, "So, what do you do?"

I'm smiling. I hope you can feel it. The question was simple enough and so was the answer—so I thought. The life I lived to get to the answer, resulting in an epiphany that came to me as headlights cast floating caterpillars into my masked vision while I drove home that night, was not so simple. That answer was cloaked in pain. The answer I gave him was easy and free and made me feel important.

"What I do," I told him, leaning across the table and lightly tapping him on the back of the arm for emphasis, "is function as the Director of 504 and Special Population Services for Metro Nashville Public Schools. In addition, I am an adjunct professor at Belmont University. I am on the leadership committee for a non-profit organization that raises awareness for the sexually abused, and I speak at engagements where we provide both mental and physical aid to those who have been impacted by abuse." He knew part of my history, and I could see through his raised eyebrows and slightly pursed lips he was impressed.

But that night on the drive home, I knew I wasn't here to impress. I was here to tell a story, my own, and the story of so many others. His question probed so deeply into my spirit. My answer to his question was what I *do*. My answer for me is who *I am*. I am a surrogate. I am a voice, indeed.

Let me explain. I love my job because I love my people. My people are students who need special assistance due to physical, mental, financial, or emotional difficulties. My team and I work to ensure students receive the best opportunity to succeed, despite any roadblocks in the way.

I take this portion of my responsibility very seriously as I have firsthand experience with educational disruption. Over the course of eighteen months, I attended four schools, and now I fight for students to have minimal disruptions and endless possibilities. So, yes, I use my voice to speak for those who need it most. They need a voice, "one crying in the wilderness" and in the conference room, the boardroom, the back room, and the principal's office. "Make straight the way for this child. For he or she is a son and daughter unlike any other, loved, cherished, and worthy of our affection and adoration," is my cry. And I make it happen. I am a voice for these students, indeed.

Voiceless

Gosh, it's terrible to lose your voice. All that pent-up energy inside tries to break the jail cell imprisoning your message. Your vocal cords mock you, yet you still try to speak. I understand. I too have lost my voice yet yearned to speak only a whisper that someone . . . I too have wanted to speak but didn't have the words to say . . . I too have been...

The problem with losing my voice wasn't the inability to speak, it was the inability to be heard. That's what abuse does. Abuse teaches we are invisible—that we can't be heard. And that is why I hate it.

Abuse, if given power, is more polarizing than racism. At least racism allows people to see color. Abuse makes us invisible. Nothing in our country seems more divisive than racism, but let me paint you a story where abuse severed a victim's ability to cry, rendered her hidden rather than visible, and left her voiceless.

It's dark, and you're a woman walking through a parking garage. The sound of two thin heels click against the concrete—stilettos, you're sure of it—as a dingy, overhead bulb flickers. You glance to the left and you spot a woman, a career woman, a career black woman, walking your way in a tight skirt with her powerful hips swaying. *She must have escaped the hood. She's probably just dressed that way to cover her lack of education. Maybe she slept her way into her position.* On and on the inner monologue continues while you size up her hair, nails, makeup, jewelry, all in less than a second. You don't like her. She's black.

You glance to the left and you spot a man with beady eyes and shifty feet. Clearly, he is not in harm's way: he is harm personified. *I have to warn her,* you think. *She's a woman, and he'll get her, or me. I need to stop her, and we'll walk out of here together.* You have to help her. She's a woman.

But you have been abused in your past, so you think, *I have to escape. He'll get me. I can't stop him. I have to get out of here.* The heels continue clicking and you see the career black woman in a tight skirt, her powerful hips swaying, and bright blue nails. *I can't help her. I have to escape, or I'll give myself to him. She'll have to escape on her own.*

The prior abuse was more polarizing than racism because the abuse prevented our imaginary friend from seeing the way of escape was *together*. She felt the need to hide, rather than help the woman. And in many cases, gender usually supersedes color. Not so for our imaginary friend. Only, this isn't just imaginary.

Many victims have suffered needless tragedies due to the color of their skin. They were treated as subhuman, often as *chattle*—less than cattle. I'm not saying that one woman would never allow another woman to be abused based on racism. History would hold me guilty for penning that. What I am saying is that we need to see each other as men and women regardless of race, but abuse makes that so much more difficult.

Abuse makes the slave and the master both seemingly subhuman to each other. Abuse solidifies racism, classism, sexism, and all other biases. Slavery is created through abuse. Our precious lady, the one whom we imagined ourselves to be just a few moments ago, couldn't dignify another lady in harm's way due to her previous abuse. She could not dignify herself. She became self-centered, even in her thoughts of sacrifice. She lost her voice; she didn't believe she could be heard.

Voices

I used to hear voices. I used to hear voices in my head: the ones telling me I wasn't good enough, the ones telling me I deserved this abuse, the ones that repeated other people's telling me I was worthless. Clearly, I have suffered my share of abuse, and I'll tell you about that later, but for now, let's focus on positive voices.

Positive voices sound as whispers in your ear, tickling as you hear them, floating like butterflies and landing in your heart, convincing you of love; voices that rip through commotion and hesitancy like an EpiPen, injecting you with courage and inspiration to fight the allergies of apathy and disdain; voices of encouragement that hold you warmly while propping you back up on your feet. I am one of those voices, and I learned it from other voices—those life whisperers.

Currently, I am pursuing public speaking, more on the motivational end of the spectrum. My goal is to turn my side hustle into a hope injector, inspiring listeners toward silencing the negative voices and embracing the positive ones. One of the recurring life whispers I hear is, "He who is in you is greater than he who is in the world" (1 John 4:4). I have met many of this world, many monsters with friendly faces, but I have also met He who lives in me. And He is greater. He is a life whisperer.

Yet I still hear negative voices. One that screams at me often says, "Anybody can talk about hope, but you'll never do anything about it!" Then he uses my own Bible against me . . . "Let us not love in word or in talk but in deed . . ." (1 John 3:18). He tries to convince me that I am all talk, a voice only.

Don't worry! I am an old pro at this, and you are too. Let me show you. When I *say*, "Give this student a chance to learn with what he has and quit asking him to dig a ditch with a spoon while everyone else uses a spade," I've *done* something. Then when I *demand*, "At least give him a small box garden to dig through with that spoon. Let him make something grow with what he has," now I've followed through. I've *made* a difference.

A foreman builds a house by using plans and giving his workers instructions. He uses his voice to facilitate his good deeds. Words are powerful, and just like someone else from long ago did, I use positive words to combat the negative voices. When a voice screams, "Let us not love in word," I respond, "Therefore encourage one another and build one another up" (1 Thessalonians 5:11), and "Pray for one another, that you may be healed" (James 5:16). Words have power, and that is why we have to be a voice for the voiceless, so they can be *heard*.

Deeds

Working with children who have special needs or adult women and men who have been sexually abused makes it seem like I am doing all of this wonderful work to help people. And I am, but that's not the point. The point is to help them be heard and to help them do good deeds too. It's not about me; it is about us. We all know it is easier to find the path when there is a trail of breadcrumbs to follow. Just like the lead runner in a marathon cuts through the wind and ultimately loses the race just to help those who follow behind, we must be willing to make a way for others—so they can follow.

Please, whatever you do, don't let yourself confine deeds to a little playground where they only help people by *doing something nice for them*. I've made that mistake. Rather, do something dangerous for them, and teach them to do something *dangerous*. Deeds are not children. They cannot be coddled and protected; they must be allowed to run freely into dangerous minefields where collateral damage is guaranteed. I could become that collateral damage based on what I've said, but I *will* be that collateral damage if I do nothing.

Forgiveness

Forgiving is a deed, but sometimes you have to voice it. Several years ago, I was chained to hatred. A man abused me when I was young. He violated me until I was deranged and detached. My body would seize up just to think about him, and I could feel my pulse racing down my clenched jawline and up into my eyes. Hate owned me. But I forgave. I read, prayed, sang, and begged to be able to forgive this man. Finally, one night I left puddles of tears and hatred on the floor in prayer. When I stood, the tears and hatred remained, but I walked away. My forgiveness was a deed.

Sometimes deeds need to be done *to* people and not *for* people. Several years after I forgave the man who sexually violated me, I had a brief encounter with him. Grief-stricken, I was attending my brother's funeral at the cemetery. My brother, Daron, had died violently in the front passenger seat of a car. My emotional gauge rocketed past the orange warning section right into the danger zone.

Inside the casket lay my little brother, his body broken from the car wreck. Unsuspectingly, he had sat in my uncle's car just before his death. They had pulled into the corner store, and my uncle asked, "Hey, you want anything?"

"No," Daron replied. Classic Daron—he didn't want to cause anybody any extra trouble. My uncle pushed into the corner store, past the ringing bell hanging above the door, and heard a jolting crunch when the door swung to a close. As did Daron's life. The car was hit from behind—drunk driver.

A week later, Momma walked onto the nearly plastic cemetery grass before me. A strong woman, she had been crippled momentarily with the pain of losing another child. In the car, waiting with a fierce gaze and a protective heart was a long-time, dear friend, No Name (I'll explain more about his name later), who had come half at my request and half out of his desire to protect me from my past, from my assailant. With an imaginary tether between my friend in the car, me, and Momma, I tucked in behind her and walked to the gravesite. And then I saw him—the monster with the friendly face.

His black suit hung from his age-weakened body and sagged around his shoulders. His face sagged too, as if it were pulling away from his bloodshot eyes for fear of infestation. His eyes slowly rolled in my direction and flashed with recognition as I marched right up to him. I stood inches from his face and looked through his clouded eyes, and I heard myself say, "I remember everything you did to me vividly, and I forgive you." While the last of the words escaped my mouth and hung in the air like a spiraling feather, I did not wait for a reaction. My arms wrapped around him and I squeezed him close. He stood statuesque and brittle, but I didn't care. His eyes glossed over, staring at nothing.

I started to turn away, but I was blindsided by a slap so refreshing it almost stole my breath away. The slap was a thought that raced through my mind and into my heart. *Even in all his fiendishness, God still loves him.*

Forgiveness erased my hatred and gave my abuser a way past his self-condemnation. The forgiveness was a deed. The words I spoke into his ears and heart were deeds, and walking away to allow him his dignity and privacy was a deed. Forgiveness allowed me to love in truth.

I am a surrogate. I stand in to absorb some pain and to speak for those who are not being heard.

I am a voice, indeed.

Teaching Voice

"Teaching is not the transference of knowledge from one person to another; teaching is loving enough to transfer all you have so another can become all she can be."-M.I.

Graduation day! Not just any graduation day, but the completion of the doctoral program at Tennessee State University in Nashville. Today I would receive my Doctor of Education (Ed.D). My mother finally came. She hadn't been there for my college graduation from Fisk, my master's at Lipscomb, or my Ed.S. from Tennessee State University, but that day she was here.

I heard my name and I glided across the stage like an air-hockey disk. I walked on air. In the crowd, my husband, David, sat with Momma and some family friends. I could see his head above the rest of the crowd and the illuminating grin on his face. Only a few more steps, and I could get out of this uncomfortable robe.

And then I fell. I fell into the trap of thinking that this day would continue without a hiccup and that all would be blessed. It's a funny thing to be awarded for your educational pursuits and to be operating in your own naivety at the same time. The fall was short-lived. A few short hours later, we opened our home for a graduation party—when the ball dropped.

Several of my friends circled around me while I leaned against a table holding punch and cake. Some knew of my formidable past, while others congratulated me for finishing what I had started. Was I arrogant? Yes. Did I need to learn something that day? Yes. But it wasn't wrong for me to enjoy the company of my friends or to celebrate my success in school. The only thing that was wrong was dropping the ball. And Momma let that happen.

During the party, Momma began to stay more and more attached to me. Like a toddler afraid to break free from her mother's skirts, Momma started to cling to me. *Awkward* doesn't describe it. Her behavior was uncanny. Never an affectionate woman, she began to hang all over me. I heard her refer to me as "My Shree," and that was disconcerting. Flattering, but weird.

My mother is a strong, resilient woman herself. She has been involved with bikers since 1993. My grandmother, Marie, even introduced her to the black biker group the Chosen Few. Grandma quit hanging with the bikers long ago, but my mother met her long-time boyfriend, Memphis, there and has been a rider ever since. My mother knows her share of struggles and deprivation, loaded with sorrow and loss. But she doesn't share.

The day I told her I had been raped at the age of nineteen, she clutched and held onto her feelings as if they were her dearest possession. I was twenty-two at the time, attending Fisk University in Nashville, and I finally opened up. Our conversation had been polite and superficial, but then I began to cry. I felt in my heart I should tell her. I said, "Momma, I have something to tell you." She glanced over curiously, but the downward slant of her eyes communicated more than just piqued curiosity. As I selectively unraveled the story of his horrid touch and vile breath, she stiffened noticeably, and then slouched forward, deflated. I finished my retelling and she looked at me but never said a word. She stood and walked out of the room, brushing past me as if I were a featherless angel—a disappointment. Momma never said a word. We never discussed it. She couldn't handle the pain, nor could she share her feelings. She couldn't share . . . "My Shree."

Please don't misunderstand. When I was much younger, I told Momma about being abused, and she acted immediately. She sought medical attention, she took me to speak with the police, she had our family friend pray over me. That was for my protection. Momma fought to protect me, but she didn't know how to share with me.

The party continued to unfold and the smiling faces passed by like jingling bells on Clydesdale horses. She stuck with me, right off my hip. She made it hard to breathe. The ball had dropped and shattered on the floor and I was still trying to figure out what pieces to pick up and who pulled the strings. *Who was this person pretending to be my mother?* Never had I seen her behave like this. The fall was over, I was back on my feet, and somewhat humiliated I had childishly believed the day would pass in perfection. My body sensed something was amiss, but my heart wouldn't tell me what it was. *Why was Momma acting so strange?*

Jealousy and inadequacy are like two violent, co-dependent lovers who can never get enough love or spite. Momma had both. She was jealous of all the powerful women in my life, speaking into me, encouraging me, loving me. Her body language, the constant clutching, the off-hand comments, and her saying, "My Shree," told me so. She also felt inadequate. She hadn't been there when I was attended college. She had abandoned me when I was nineteen. Momma, without her daughter's approval, felt exposed.

A candlestick fire lights a room brilliantly and beautifully, but a house fire consumes and destroys—leaving only a trail of ashes. A fire is never satisfied, but it can be tamed. So it was the same with my mother's desire for approval. She was burning everything up around her in her quest for affirmation as a mother. I was already proud of her. I already respected her. I already accepted her. I had to tell her, so she could burn like a candle is supposed to, only at the wick.

Right then, I asked her to step into the other room. It's a funny thing to be the child taking your mother into the other room—ironic. The room awkwardly embraced us in quiet confidence. I can still hear the enthusiastic chitter-chatter of my friends beyond the wall as I mouthed the words to mother, "I love you. I am proud of you. I respect you. You are my mother. Don't let what you see in these other women here get in the way of who you are and who I am to you. You are my mother and I respect you for who you are."

As the last few words rolled from my lips, Momma, my strong Momma, leaned on my shoulder and cried. Her cry wasn't the wail of a heart-wrenched parent; it was the silent relief of forgotten failure falling in teardrops and spattering on the floor. It's a touching thing to wipe away your mother's tears—ironic, but lovely. My mother was an angel with scars.

That day I did not give my mother anything but, once again, ironically, I taught her something. I did not give her a voice; I taught her about voice. See, Momma always loved me, but she didn't always know how to show it. She had traveled so far to see me, and she was still wounded by the times she hadn't. Her actions showed me she loved me, and my actions showed her that I respected and loved her. But it wasn't enough until I voiced my respect, and, then, we learned about voice together.

But monsters were still in the closet.

Finding Voice

"Will you marry me? I want you to be mine, forever."—Unknown

From nearly as far back as I can remember, monsters have always existed. From nearly as recently as I can forget, there have always been angels. And the memories started and ended with men. As you can assume, I have had my trouble with them. Boy, have I. I am a strong, independent, attractive, African-American woman, and I have a fatal flaw—I like men. But, sometimes, they hated me.

When I was a child, I was sexually abused. The abuse caused a lot of scarring, emotional and physical, and those monsters followed me most of my life. Not the monsters who abused me: the monsters that came with the abuse—doubt, fear, loneliness, and perfectionism. I'll get to the monsters, but for now I want to discuss the healing. I couldn't tell this story without the healing, and I couldn't heal until I found another piece of my voice.

The first time David proposed, I didn't find anything but frustration and a little laughter. David, my husband, is an interesting man. He comes from a family quite different than mine, and his sense of humor and romance, well . . . different. His dad was funny, so I am not so sure how the apple fell so far away from the tree. Maybe it just rolled—right into my lap.

David grew up with his mother, Ella, and his father, Reginald, just like the Huxtables. His dad was an honest, hard-working man, and his mom was a gentle, loyal, loving soul even during her last days with dementia. The day I met them, I hadn't known David for long, and I was breathing heavily and sweaty-palmed, but I came bearing gifts.

David and I met by chance. I had purchased a home in Nashville, and at thirty-five years old, I was as giddy as a little girl. One of my best girlfriends Tanisha told me about her friend who could help me move. I was at her house when she told me about her friend David, and he just happened to be on his way over. Just "happened" to be . . . but, I'm not the kind of girl to sit and around and wait for a man, and I had boxes to move, so I started to leave before David arrived. When I stepped into the driveway, a car whipped in next to mine. I can't tell you what color the car was that day, but I can tell you the man who got out of the car sure got my attention—but I didn't let him know that.

I played it cool, and we exchanged numbers, then I was on my way. I had things to move, but something had moved me, just a little bit. David and I kept in contact over the phone through the following months and met up one night when he returned from the Essence Festival in New Orleans. We met at the airport in Nashville, pulled out onto Murfreesboro Road, and headed north on our first date.

My palms were never sweaty when I hung out with David. I was cool, and so was our time. We were so relaxed together. We had dinner that night at a local Mexican restaurant; I guess you could say that we started dating that day. And we've never stopped.

Our relationship hasn't been perfect or easy, but it has been an adventure, and it has been fun, which is why I was so nervous about meeting his parents. I was afraid the adventure would end, that in front of his parents he would open the treasure box he had discovered, but they would only see fool's gold.

You see, David and I spent our time relaxing, talking, and laughing together. We were relaxed, stress-free. He would come visit me at my new home, and we would sit around and talk for hours about everything and nothing. I would tell him about my students and my dreams and even read him some of my poetry. He would tell me about basketball, his goals, and his son. Those were special days, but meeting the Huxtables, that would be different—they might find him a fool.

Giving Voice

I love giving gifts. The way that someone's smile will light up or the gleam in her eye is more than enough reason for me to give somebody a gift. But these were David's parents. I was a nomad. They were . . . normal. Now, I am a pretty confident girl, but we all have our fears, and one of mine had always been meeting my friend's parents. This was magnified by ten million. David told me that his dad loved orange slice candy and peanuts. Those were his two favorite foods. David didn't just offer up that information; I had to ask.

On the evening we were supposed to meet David's parents, I picked up a few bags of orange slice candy and some peanuts. I think I had every flavor and type of peanut possible in that grocery cart. I learned that some stores even carry jelly-flavored peanuts. There I was, pushing around a cart filled with peanuts and candy, with a deranged look on my face—I needed to hurry. I am sure the girl at the checkout counter thought I was pregnant or had the munchies.

I raced back home in time to freshen up and to look cool and nimble when David picked me up. My heart felt otherwise. David carried in the cake and flowers I had bought for his mother, and I carried in the candy and the peanuts. His dad met us at the door, and I felt my face blush red. Quickly, I offered him my gift—staying cool.

He saw it, looked me square in the eye, and said, "Are you trying to bribe me?"

I said, "So what if I am?"

The orange slice candy wrapping caught his attention, and I showed him the peanuts. A small grin emerged on this face curling up into dimples, and he looked at me sideways through those kind eyes and said, "You are alright by me!"

My gift had given me a place, right there in their heart. I was accepted, and I didn't see any monsters—only angels.

Ella was an angel. She had dementia, a monster of a disease. Racking your personality and memory, dementia eats away at you until you forget your family, your friends, yourself. Piece by piece it takes you away and tries to steal the peace from those around you. But it couldn't break Ella's wings. She just soared right through it.

She thought my name was Kelly. I'm smiling now just thinking about it. I guess my little dimple is starting to show too. I'd stop by their house in my BMW and we would go out for long drives with the top down and the radio up. Usually on these dates we'd listen to Aretha Franklin or the Temptations, snapping our fingers as the wind blew around our smiling faces. We would sing and laugh and embrace the day as it came to us. That is how I remember Ella, smiling, laughing, calling me Kelly, and soaring above the clouds. However, I did see her get snarky once.

She snipped the day after David "proposed" to me—if I can even call it that. We were driving down an old country road near the outskirts of Nashville, out toward Bellevue, when he popped the question. On our way to a basketball game that he would be refereeing, David pulled the car over to the side of the road and said, "Will you marry me?"

I said, after a long pause, "You are not ready for marriage right now!" smiling slyly. And that was the end of the conversation. Sure, David gave me grief over rejecting him, and I made fun of him for the worst proposal ever—I didn't know the next one would be even worse—but we didn't really discuss it any further. He had asked, and I knew he wasn't ready, so I didn't take it seriously. Neither did Ella.

The next day, David tried to embarrass me in front of his mother. He told her the story of the proposal, hamming it up, and making it abundantly clear that I had crushed his poor, little heart with my rejection. His mom wasn't too lucid at this time, and she did a lot of incoherent talking to herself, but when David told her about my refusal, she had to defend her Kelly.

She looked right at David and said, "*That* doesn't sound like a proposal to me!" and she went back to mumbling a bit to herself. I tried to stifle my grin, but I couldn't. I laughed and laughed and laughed at David's expense. I knew Ella was an angel all along—an archangel. I could tell by the inverted arches she created, curling up into dimples on both mine and Reginald's faces. I had tried to give her a voice on our "dates," and she gave me laughter and a smile.

Finding Voice

Although David's first proposal was a colossal blunder, he managed to do even worse the second time. That day was one unlike any other, that is for sure. And the night started that way too.

Earlier in the day, David had called me. Something was up, and I was trying to figure it out. He was talking, but he wasn't making any sense. His words made sense, but his message didn't.

"Shree, I love you. I can't stand our time apart. You're too busy. I don't want to keep going on like this—playing second fiddle to your life and career. I don't have time for these games; you mean too much to me. I don't have time for this relationship. I can't keep going on like this," he babbled.

"What are you saying, David?" He was almost incoherent. I could feel my lips start to purse and my eyes begin to cut. My ears popped as I forced out a sigh of exasperation and pain. The trust monster was back.

The trust monster, whose name is Doubt, is the opposite of the angel of trust. Parading around like a wise scholar, never subject to naivety, the trust monster masks himself in cynicism and defensiveness. He is cloaked in darkness, and he had crept in through the darkness and buried his dagger deep in my heart years before. The trust monster tells me I can't trust angels—and never men.

David was wrong. I didn't have other higher priorities that competed with him. I just had my passions, the same passions he loved about me, and the same passions I had shared with him since we first met. He was conflicted, and I was right.

I am a major advocate of self-talk. For me, it is one of the most important life skills. With positive self-talk, we can convince ourselves of our true worth and move mountains. That night, I forgot to talk to myself, and I just listened. I listened to my doubts and fears, and they told me I was unworthy and that David was scum. I needed somebody to trust.

My father talked in codes—words that vaguely represented what he wanted to say but disguised the true meaning of his message—and I hated it, so David had crossed two lines. One, he was breaking my heart. Two, he reminded me of my father with his ambiguity. I probably would have cut him if he had been close to me, but luckily for him, and me, he was on the other side of town.

I was so desperate to find someone to turn to that night, somebody to trust, so I turned to my next-door neighbor, Robert. He's kind, attractive, sensitive, middle-aged, and sincere. On this particular night, he was effusive. I came over to unburden myself and share my woes, my man troubles, with someone who would understand. Robert was there physically, but he did not seem present in the moment.

On top of Robert's home is a section with a flat roof. Sometimes he has parties up there with lots of guests. On this night, it was just Robert, his phone, and I—in that order. His phone would ring, and he would answer it, or respond to a text message. His partner, Michael, was trying to get in contact with him. Unexpectedly, Michael's dog was being euthanized. Pizza was on its way and we drank wine as the clouds overswept the moon. A gentle breeze blew and the sounds from below were of the city and the country, of people talking and leaves rustling.

Robert would lean over the side of the home and "holla" at the people below. He ran downstairs to get something. He came back up without his phone. He went back down. He came back up. The phone rang. The pizza was here; down he went again. Right back up. All the time I played Fantasia in the background, sipped on wine, and sang along, "If you don't want me, then don't talk to me . . ."

The evening started to become a blur between the chatter, the wine, the music, and Robert's erratic behavior. He was like a cat who could smell a mouse but couldn't see it. But really he was a fox—a sly one. David had been texting back and forth with Robert, making sure I was there and making sure I was good and upset. I was—two points for David.

The wine glass was at my side, the music was between my ears, and the pizza was in my lap when David showed up. He walked onto the rooftop with his son behind him and said, "Shree?"

I looked up as if he were crazy. He was crazy, or one of us was crazy. I was triggered, and then it all started to melt away. On the rooftop, David dropped to one knee and said, "Shree, will you marry me? I want you to be mine, forever."

The pause was pregnant, speechless. I bumbled out the question, "Me?" I looked around in shock. Was he talking to me? Did I deserve this? The unworthy monster had crept in silently and taken up residence, and I didn't even know it. The unworthy monster masks herself in loneliness. She must stay isolated because she is not worthy of the affection of others. She had been whispering in my ear, *You should have expected him to end it this way. You're no good.*

I looked up and I saw Robert crying. David's son was crying too. Tears crowded my eyes and rolled down my cheeks, leaving streak marks in the dark. I stood. I am sure the pizza fell somewhere in the process, but I don't remember when. And in the middle of a rooftop in Nashville, amid the smell of pizza and alcohol, through the tears and laughter of both gay and straight men, next to a cardboard box of pizza and some cheap wine, I accepted David's proposal.

The worst proposal ever.

To this day, David still brags about his proposal to his friends. His plan to get me upset, and then propose had worked. Even though I said yes, I still don't think it was cool or romantic. *Sigh.*

One of my monsters, the unworthy monster, died that night. And I found a little more voice. I don't mean to say that I didn't have a voice before David, I did. I had a strong one. But on that night, I found a little deeper voice. The voice that comes from being accepted, pursued, loved by another. I guess I found another angel with scars—David.

The funny thing is I always thought that angels couldn't have children, but it turns out I was wrong. Ella was an angel, and after she passed on and went to heaven, David, her son, became my new angel. And we both have scars.

Following Voice

"For I know the plans I have for you, declares the LORD, plans for welfare and not for evil, to give you a future and a hope."–Jeremiah 29:11

I haven't forgotten the other two monsters, fear and perfectionism; they just weren't as significant on the day David proposed. I hate them, and I can feel them right now. Today, I have to follow a voice because following that voice is the only way I have been able to overcome the fear monster and the inadequacy monster.

I don't believe hearing voices is crazy. Sure, some maladies cause people to hear voices that are figments of their imaginations; however, if you believe in the supernatural, you might just believe that *real*, intelligible voices *are* speaking. I hear voices. They are not audible voices, but I still hear voices. I hear voices from the past, I hear my own voice, I hear the monsters' voices: doubt, fear, inadequacy, and unworthiness, and I hear God's voice. This presents two distinct problems. The first is discerning who is talking. The second is choosing to whom I am going to listen. Not to the monsters, anymore.

I followed a voice a few months ago, in September 2017, when I spoke at the Tennessee Social Worker's Conference; I believe it was

God prompting me to speak. I heard it, I felt it, and I know it. I first discovered God's voice through reading. I can remember the first time I read Isaiah 45:2, "I will go before you and level the exalted places, I will break in pieces the doors of bronze and cut through the bars of iron." Surely, I didn't believe it. You don't have to either, but over time, I came to believe it.

I fell in love with Bible reading around the age of fifteen, but even more so as I grew older. Searching through the Scriptures for hours became a pastime I enjoyed immensely. Specific words and phrases such as "I will restore to you the years that the swarming locust has eaten" (Joel 2:25) would descend on me and resonate. Imperatives such as "Be still, and know that I am God" (Psalm 46:10a) were passionate, comforting commands to me. Remember, I had been sexually abused as a child, inappropriately touched as a young teen, and raped at nineteen. Imperatives from men were typically hateful and harmful, with their pleasure and my pain the only things in mind. Now, I had a source of comfort.

This is not an argument against your belief system, this is not a plea to get you to convert, and this is not a self-righteous moment where I write about my relationship with God. This is my presentation of how I process the voices around me, how I have heard God's voice, and how I conquered some monsters at the close of the Tennessee Social Workers' Conference. This is me being me.

Blocking Voices

As part of my occupation in Support Services, I work with many social workers. One of the engineers of the conference from the Tennessee Association of School Social Workers was familiar with my story. The theme for that year was "Champions of Social Change," and she thought I would be "a great fit" as the closing keynote speaker. The night before the conference, I wasn't so sure. I could not sleep. The fear monster was in my bedroom, whispering. I didn't know if I would be able to do it. Could I dredge up all the emotional pain in front of an audience? Could I scrape the dregs of my shame and face the rejection of hundreds of individuals? Luckily, David was in the room too, but at this time, I felt alone in my own thoughts.

I had to block the voices. The questions were of doubt and fear, and they did not produce good things in me. The fear monster plays off the inadequacy monster, and the inadequacy monster's name is

Perfectionism. And she is a female, always a female. Perfectionism asks questions that can only be answered by admitting a failure or shortcoming. *How will you speak to this group considering your past failures? How will you convince them you're qualified? Why would they listen to someone who is so weak, a woman, and black? How will you do it without enough sleep? Why are you nervous if you're so strong?* Her game is a game of concession: if she can get us to concede that we're inadequate, that we first have brokenness to overcome, we will focus only on our weaknesses.

My favorite poet, Atticus, wrote, "She wore a thousand faces all to hide her own," (Atticuspoetry) which is exactly what I wanted to do. Replacing my face with my mask of resolve or strength seemed like the only wise thing to do. Except, it wasn't. The wise thing to do was to identify the source of my pain—fear of failure, fear of rejection (atelophobia)—and to follow a different voice. I identified the source, chose not to listen or answer her questions, and blocked her voice. But that wasn't enough.

Replacing Voices

I didn't figure it all out that night. I replaced the voices by talking to David, reading to myself, talking to myself, and listening to and praying to God. The butterflies remained. Buried in my abdomen and fluttering about in my chest, the butterflies of nervousness kept me uneasy.

We left the house early. We drove to the conference center, and I was in severe pain. My pain wasn't physical, although it manifested itself physically—I could feel it. My pain was emotional. At the conference, I would have to reveal some of my scars. I would undress my wounds and present them, but I would have to pretend that I was content with them. I am not. I have peace about them now, but I am not content with them because they still cause me pain.

Fear, anger, and resentment all arise from pain, and here I was about to bring out my painful past, so others could understand we don't always see everyone's scars on the outside. Most times, the scars are hidden. A few times I nearly doubled over in the car. I wasn't trying to be dramatic, it just hurt.

David and I arrived about two hours early, so I could prepare for the speech. I began to walk around the conference center, speaking to myself. I waged an internal argument with my fear and my inadequacy.

My heart quickened. My breathing deepened. My eyes closed and my temples bore out the constant drumming sound of my pulse. I was sinking.

Following Voice

But . . . I am a pretty resilient girl. The monsters chased me, gnashing their teeth and stomping their feet, and I couldn't hide behind a masked face to disarm a real predator. I had to become truly connected with who I was and put on a different type of armor. So I spoke, and my declaration was a cry for help, a request, a calling out for a superior message.

I prayed, "Teach me what must be said in this hour. Teach me what must be said in this hour," over and over again as I paced the floor of the empty conference room until I started to calm down and the sweat began to dissipate. I listened.

I can't tell you exactly what I felt after that, but I can paraphrase it and give you the result. I heard, I heard something like what I already believed. I heard I was called to do this, I was created to do this. I heard I was responsible for speaking out for others who could not speak for themselves. In my pain, in my weaknesses, others would become stronger—I would become stronger. I heard that I was no longer voiceless and that I had found my voice and I needed to follow His voice. I did not hear an audible voice, but I did feel a confirmation of the Scriptures I had read and the drive I had felt. I needed to be a voice for the voiceless and speak out.

So, I did. As Atticus wrote, "She conquered her demons [monsters] and wore her scars like wings" (Atticuspoetry). I spoke to a crowd of many and infused them with the confidence that we can make a difference. That we, together, need to protect those little angels with scars and use our own scars to teach them to become angels with scars and wings.

For my speech, I received a standing ovation. The applause felt good, and, honestly, I wanted to hold on to that momentary glory, but I couldn't. I was filled with gratitude. I had been covered in fear, but One who is not fearful said to me, "Be strong and courageous. Do not be frightened" (Joshua 1:9), and I listened. He said, "Fear not, for I am with you" (Isaiah 41:10), and I followed suit.

I can never be perfect, so to beat the inadequacy monster and all her perfectionist questioning, I have to follow the voice of someone who is. I can't be fearless, so to beat the fear monster, I have to follow the voice of someone who walked through fear to bear my pain for me. He has scars. He has scars on both His hands and His feet. He has a scar on His side, and He is better than any angel I've ever met. I chose to block my own and others' negative voices, replace them with good voices, and follow the best one. Even the monsters tremble.

Leading Voices

"Watch carefully, the magic that occurs when you give a person just enough comfort to be themselves."–Atticus

Before I ever spoke at a Social Worker's Conference, before I represented thousands of students in middle Tennessee academically, I had the opportunity to test my leadership voice in the life of a girl named Jessica. I met her in 2007, while I lived in Nashville and taught at Hillsboro High School. I'll explain how Jessica and I became acquainted momentarily, but first, I want to point out the poetic nature of our relationship. As you may have noticed, I like poetry.

Often, life can be poetic. Through its pitfalls and heartbreak and its ascendancy to high mountains of euphoria, life can be poetic. The poetry of life may be rhythmic and effortless or harsh, choppy, blunt. Cycles perpetuate cycles, seasons come and go, babies are born and awaken the world with the cry of life, and mothers die despite the painful cries and needs of their children. Yet I still like life, and I still like poetry. Sometimes life is poetic, and the broken are given the voice to lead the shattered, and the shattered receive the voice to lead the world.

I wrote this poem, "Yesterday," before I met my friend Jessica:
As I am sitting here, I am in a state of confusion.

I don't have a problem with being here,
But I have a problem with being here in this state of be-
ing—
I have no control. I'm concerned with my well-being. I'm
lost.
I feel like a bird tryin' to be freed.
Freed from this cage I placed myself in.
I'm afraid of dyin', I'm afraid of quitting, I'm afraid of
failure.
I don't know what to do. I feel lost. I wish I had the an-
swers,
I wish I knew what was on the other side of this state
here.
I pray that I am freed.
Freed from this place and to let it be memory.
A reminder of doing things in the now, and not, "I will
tomorrow."
Or, "I should have yesterday."
But I will today, today,
Live out my dreams
And make no more commitments without commitment.
I pray for security and protection.
I want to begin again and take nothing for granted
And stay committed to God's purpose for me.

As Robert Hayden so eloquently wrote, "What did I know, / What
did I know" about getting what I asked for?

Songs often have leaders. There are lead singers, song leaders, lead
guitarists, lead vocalists, and there are those who follow. Poetry is the
same. Our lives are like poems, we write them: sometimes we learn to
write them by following, and sometimes by leading. My life became
more poetic when I learned to stay committed to God's purpose for
me, to follow when I ought to follow, to lead when I ought to lead, and
to be a voice, indeed. And Jessica really needed one.

I met Jessica and her smiling face but sad eyes as she descended from a Greyhound bus into the shadow of my cousin, Marky. Marky, my cousin from L.A., moved to Nashville to get a fresh start on life, and he brought Jessica with him. I wasn't expecting her, and she was surely following the wrong leader. The wrong voice was leading her.

Our meeting was caused by events that occurred years before—by death—first my brother Daron's, and then my cousin Woodah's. The tragic deaths of my brother and my cousin pushed my family to reconsider priorities in their lives. My cousin Marky made it a priority to get out of L.A. I believe Marky's relationship with Daron and Woodah pushed him to want to run away, but I believe the timing and nature of their deaths scared him even more. My brother was killed on November 19, 2005, by a drunk driver, as I wrote earlier. My cousin, Woodah, was murdered on May 19, 2006. With only six months between their deaths, and the fact they acted like brothers, the pain was too close for Marky. He lost part of himself when they died.

Woodah died a senseless death. He stood in front of the house tinkering on his car. With the hood propped open, his head crooked down, and his body cast over the engine, he was extremely vulnerable. The car wasn't running, so the only sounds in the street were the sounds of other vehicles passing by and a few occasional voices. A car turned onto the street, and the sound of the tires crunching concrete was probably the last thing Woodah heard before the gunshots and his own screams ripped the sky.

Woodah's car was red, but he lived in a Crip neighborhood. The primary color for the Crips is blue, and the color red signifies the color of the Bloods, the rival gang. Woodah wasn't in a gang, but he was under the hood of a red car in the wrong neighborhood at the wrong time, when manliness was on the line.

The boy driving the other vehicle was undergoing his first gang initiation test. He had to kill a Blood, and he had to do it quickly. It's kind of like a rite of passage from boyhood into manhood, but it only perpetuates the belief that men cause pain and can't be trusted. When they are killing others, they are really killing themselves.

Shot after senseless shot discharged bullet after bullet into Woodah's unsuspecting, and then falling body. Auntie Bailey heard the shots being fired and tried to rush down the concrete stairs, scraping her knees and legs, to her son, but as she collapsed down the stairs, his body fell lifeless, riddled with eight bullet holes, thudding upon the ground. The sound of the poetry of life was blunt, traumatic, harsh, like hot flesh slapping hot pavement in the wake of crashing cymbals—bullet shells bouncing and rolling away. As his blood poured out on the street, the end of his life didn't feel poetic, it felt like two concrete blocks smashing together with your finger between them.

After the death of his two cousins, Marky decided to get out. He phoned me in Nashville and asked if he could come stay. Of course, I had already had conversations with his mother and family. I was torn apart by the loss my aunt felt over her son, Woodah. I was torn by the loss I felt. I was torn that men were trying to heal their own scars by causing others. So was Marky. He needed a new environment, a fresh start, and I had had some success in Nashville, so I told him to come on.

Marky is an odd one. He felt safer riding a Greyhound bus than he did flying on a plane. Maybe it wasn't just how he felt, but that he could bring his girlfriend along without telling anybody if he took a Greyhound. And that is exactly what he did. He jumped on a Grey-hound and brought Jessica with him. The only problem was that nobody told me. Even when he arrived, nobody *told* me—I was left to figure it out.

Marky came off the bus with Jessica in tow, and I didn't even realize they were together. He didn't introduce her, we just . . . met. I started to put the pieces together that *they* were together and hadn't met on the bus, so I had to make a quick decision. I only had a one-bedroom apartment. My plan had been to help Marky get up on his feet while he stayed with me, and then help him find a new apartment. Now, I might have to get a new apartment of my own.

There wasn't any time for all the future predicting; I had to make my decision. So I listened. In that quick moment of prayer, I did not hear a voice, yet I knew in my spirit I was being called to let them stay. Again, I listened. Those two senseless deaths from years before were the reason I met Jessica and the reason I listened.

We drove back to my apartment in my cloth-top Jeep, Jessica sitting in the back. She was a beautiful girl, gorgeous. She looked like a California beauty, a "'round-the way girl," but something was missing in her eyes. Through the rearview mirror as I talked and gazed, I saw that her eyes were sad and she needed a leader. Who knew it would be me?

Speaking Voice

People can't hear your teaching voice until they learn to trust your speaking voice. That is what I had to learn with Marky and with

Jessica. We drove back to my one-room apartment, and we set them up with some space.

They stayed for about a year. In that year, I learned a few things about Jessica, Marky, and myself. My job at the time was to teach at Jere Baxter Alternative Learning Center. My educational pursuit was to complete my master's degree in special education at Lipscomb University, but my purpose was to guide this young girl into adulthood.

During the time they stayed with me, they both worked at McDonald's. They worked and paid bills, and Jessica started going back to school to get her high school diploma. They had some relationship issues, but the problems didn't seem too major at first, until they got out of control.

Marky started to decline. He quit paying attention to the priorities. One month, they let the cable bill slide—it was the only bill they had to pay. They learned from having it cut off. Neither took ownership of the responsibility to pay the bill, but I could see that Jessica was taking responsibility in other areas of her life. On the other hand, Marky, wasn't. He began to cheat on Jessica. He didn't keep regular hours. He lied. Then he broke federal law. He had some weed shipped straight to the house, through the U.S. Postal Service! I had to ask him to leave; he was going to destroy us.

The disappearances started, not with Marky, but with Jessica. She was like a ghost; there was a trail of her belongings, but for an entire week, I couldn't catch her. If I was home, she was gone. It was clear she was evading Marky and avoiding me. She didn't want to go back; I knew it.

When I finally cornered her, I told her she didn't have to go back to L.A. She could stay, and that is when things really began to change. That is when I began to meet the true Jessica, not the apparition, when she began to tell me about her life—when Marky was gone.

Thirty-one years old, that is how old I was. I was probably about as emotionally intelligent as a twelve-year old, but now I had another person for whom I was responsible. I didn't have any family there either, and I had to learn the ropes on my own. I didn't feel capable to lead someone else personally at the same time, but I was going to be obedient. Let me write that again: I was going to be obedient. It wasn't going to be like "Yesterday"—I was going to take nothing for granted and stay true to God's purpose for me.

Over the next few weeks, I found out that Jessica didn't have anyone in the world to call family. Before she moved to Nashville with Marky, she had been living in his mother's garage. Before that, she lived pillar to post, and before that, she survived the foster care program. When I met her, her face was twenty-one, but her eyes spoke eternities of pain; she had been only four years old when her parents abandoned her.

Authorities searched for her parents, but no one ever found them—elusive is the heart who doesn't want to be captured by responsibility. Unsealing her records proved impossible, and she traded homes like a hand-me-down chest of drawers until legal adulthood was thrust upon her. Like a stray cat, she traipsed from tenement housing to garage parlors until she followed Marky up the steps of the eastbound Greyhound bus. Her brother, abandoned the same day as she, remained in California. Seventeen years she lived without a real family, and after Marky scattered, I tried to pick up the pieces. I spoke softly but firmly; if I tried to teach her before establishing implicit trust, the message in my words would have been filtered through her past experiences and discarded in the slush pond of wasted words. When you're worried about walking down the street without getting mugged or harassed, you don't hear the singing of the birds or the whispers of the wind; you hear the hissing of vultures and the scuttles of rats.

So, I spoke. I very matter-of-factly taught her about life. She grew in wisdom and courage over the next four years. I taught her about budgeting, boys, and beliefs. We worked though some of her troubles with her parents and her past. Negligence assaulted her heart and body, leaving her damaged both psychologically and physically, resulting in medical issues requiring surgery. I took care of her. The situation yoked me with motherhood responsibility, while making me feel childlike because I was inadequate—not sure what I was doing. I kept speaking.

Jessica kept learning. In late 2011, I facilitated her acceptance into an accelerated program where she could earn her diploma. She performed well in school and graduated in January 2012, nearly five years after we had first met. She kept working, kept paying bills, kept staying away from toxic boys, and she kept learning. She transformed into a radiant beauty, not just in her outward appearance, but through learning to love, her inward beauty emerged in that great smile and made other people feel internally significant. And then she screwed up.

Singing Voice

She left. Jessica left. I couldn't find her. She disappeared. All of her belongings remained in our apartment, but I couldn't find *her*. She never told me where she was going or when she would be back. I called her work; nobody knew where she was, and she wasn't scheduled to work for another three days anyway. I called her friends; they didn't know where she was either. One of them told me she thought Jessica was hanging out with another friend, but when I finally reached that friend, she hadn't seen Jessica in two days.

Desperation settled in. I imagined her wandering lost, or abducted, or running to her past. Maybe I pushed her too hard. Maybe I spoke too much, taught too much, exasperated her with that voice of mine. Maybe it was my fault.

After exhausting all of my efforts, I turned to the police and the hospitals. I had to find her. I pressed the number for the hospital on my phone, but before it had time to dial, I heard her key jiggle the lock. I tossed the phone down and felt my pulse rise, along with my temperature. Jessica walked through the door, nonchalantly, and happiness, relief, and anger converged in my body. I couldn't speak to her. I knew what happened, what she'd done. She didn't get lost or stolen or anything. She left without saying goodbye, telling me where she was going, or when she would be back. Nobody had cared to teach her how.

I helped her secure her own apartment. Really, it wasn't because she had left without saying when she would be home; I helped her get an apartment because we had transitioned. She finished school, and now she was grown. I stopped speaking so much, and I started singing more. I didn't begin to literally sing to her; it was more like poetry. I encouraged her by praising her efforts, and I backed off on the teaching and speaking parts. She flourished. She continued working locally until she landed a contracting job in May 2012. The job was not as a contractor/builder, but as a contractor for a private company. She was moving overseas.

I knew I would be sad to see her go, but I also knew we had a place in each other's hearts. She blossomed into a healthy, young sapling, ready to be transplanted to newer, more fertile soil. My smile broadened, my shoulders buoyed, but my heart sank, for a piece of it crossed the ocean without me. After that, she matured rapidly. She lived in Afghanistan, grew in Dubai, and flourished in the Philippines. She maximized her earning potential, capitalizing enough to buy a Lexus with cash and purchase her own home. Now, we speak internationally, and although she continues her search for her birth mom, we mother each other.

When Jessica calls, overflowing with gratitude and success stories from her life, she sings over me. Her singing voice showers me with encouragement, just as my singing voice propels her into a bright future. It's wonderful, and freeing, and spiritual all at the same time.

Life sings poetry. At times, life is blunt and harsh and leaves us lying in a pool of blood surrounded by grief, remorse, and loss. Sometimes, life blows us a kiss that whispers through the wind and leaves, rotates atop the wings of birds, and falls slowly and listlessly to the ground like a dandelion bulb, pausing just long enough to brush our cheek in its descent. Marky came to Nashville as a broken man with a broken girl, but he left as a lonely, broken man, with no girl. Jessica came to Nashville as a broken girl with a broken man, but she left as a resilient, purposeful woman, and now she leads others with her bright eyes.

A Voracious Learner

"He who says he can and he who says he can't are both usually right."–Confucius

I once heard, "A wise person does not boast of her accomplishments but allows other people to boast for her." But that's for *wise* people. Most times, it is difficult even to accept praise from other people, to allow them to boast. Is that unwise? Two affirmations, two compliments, I have repeatedly received I no longer question: learner and leveler. But I have often rejected them in the past. One of my letters of recommendation reads, "Shree is a learner," and "she has an eye for equity." As a teacher, I pride myself on building equity into how I treat all of my students, but I never considered myself a leveler, much less a learner. I fought against the compliment.

Not even as a student did I consider myself a true learner. I would wonder, *How do they get those scale model ships inside those glass bottles?* but I never looked it up. My grades fluctuated like my emotions, haphazardly. No, she must have been wrong in her recommendation. I was not a learner. I was just a hard worker.

I don't like conspiracies, and I don't like theories, but in the past something alien has seized me by the throat, pressed me against the wall, and warned, "Pay attention to me!" Conspiracy theories are frustrating, but I swear something is out there, something in the air, something that is out to get me. Is there a name for this self-conspirator? Is it apathy or depression—fate maybe? I believe hard work pays off, but only if you're not working just as hard against yourself as you are for yourself.

When I was a child, I always dreamed of being a teacher. Actually, I dreamed in threes: I wanted to be a teacher, a lawyer, and a police officer, but, primarily, a teacher. I gathered up my siblings and my cousins and we played school—I played only if I could be the teacher. During trips to the dollar store, I stocked up on school supplies, not for actual school, but for the pretend school I taught at my house. I built a curriculum, taught lessons, assigned work, all from a girl who used to cry out, "I don't wanna go to school! I don't wanna go to school!" Teaching was my first love.

Life took me off track, and I struggled to find my way back to my dream. Dreams are like that. They seem to evaporate when we lose our innocence, but they always seem to reappear as peace is being restored. Maybe that's what dreams are—our mind's conjuring when at total peace. Prior to attending Fisk University in Nashville, most of my life more closely resembled a nightmare. At times since, I've wondered if I acclimated to the nightmares—if I had been creating them.

During college, I also began pursuing the police academy. I went to the third round of testing, but a voice inside told me police work was not for me. That same voice told me I wanted to wear pumps and heels, skirts and suits to work!

Teaching enthralled me, enchanted me; I dreamed of it. After my messy childhood and adolescence, I began to avoid my dream—I thought it was too good to be true, that it was unattainable. So, I would avoid the opportunities.

I attended Fisk University from the fall of 1998 through the spring of 2003, when I graduated. After I graduated college, I did not directly pursue teaching. I self-sabotaged. Instead of pursuing a career in education, I worked some odd jobs, one of which was for Sprint. I was stalling, fearful of pursuing my dream. I worked hard to prove myself, but I also worked against myself. One day my boyfriend called and asked me to add some minutes to his phone. I don't know what I was thinking—he worked for Sprint too—but I did it! I conspired against myself, and I paid for it—I got fired.

Although losing the job at Sprint created a tremendous financial blunder, and I had mangled my reputation with my ill-advised actions, getting fired was actually inspirational. The spirit to teach was thrust back in me. Working for Sprint was my way of dodging my dream, keeping myself awake so I couldn't realize what I really wanted from my dreams. God had a way of leveling the path for me. I would never associate God with my decision to steal from Sprint; I only associate Him with the redemption from it and the fulfillment of a dream.

After getting fired by Sprint in 2003, I began substitute teaching, and I ended up at Bailey Middle School in Nashville. From the beginning, teaching felt natural. My presence in the classroom seemed innate, and by the end of the semester I had secured a job teaching at Jere Baxter Alternative School for the fall semester! Now, that was exciting, but that was also the alternative school—the alternative to regular public school—to prison. I wasn't worried, I didn't have any misgivings, I accepted reality as reality.

A Voracious Leveler

When a strong breeze blows above the ground and through the atmosphere, it doesn't make much noise on its own, but when it begins brushing against trees, around buildings, through bushes, or atop grass or sand, it creates friction—and the friction creates the noise. My first year teaching was very, very noisy. The noise was the wholesome sound of hard work, like a construction site. As I worked to level the playing field for my students, something else happened: my efforts provided my students with the best opportunity to learn as well as giving me the chaos my mind still craved. The work wasn't the chaos; the frenetic pace I kept and the expectations I created for myself were. I liked the friction. I feared the peace; peace meant quiet, or so I thought.

My first year at Jere Baxter Alternative was awesome! The population changed frequently yet maintained diversity. In the beginning, I had only boys. I had boys enrolled there for offenses such as carrying weapons, using drugs, gang-related activities, and even multiple tardies! Attendance fluctuated, students came and went—some back to the regular public school and others on to more severe places. The kids were raw and street smart. They had high non-verbal IQs, but their educations had massive gaps.

I taught math, and I clearly recall the first time I gave them an assessment. I walked into school dressed and pressed as I always did—hair done, skirt and shirt ironed and starched, heels on, nails done, and eyes wide open. The students knew what to expect; we had already connected and created that foundation. They knew I had high expectations and cared for them, and we understood the balance; trust undergirded the classroom.

The crowded musk of the room thickened in the late-August heat. The room was tense; years of pent-up aggression and anger rose to the ceiling. The slightest academic pressure made them feel uncomfortable, defensive, angry. Did they trust me? Yes. Did they respond well to pressure? Not yet. I could tell quickly that some of the students couldn't add and subtract, some couldn't multiply and divide, some could divide but not subtract, and some could only subtract. They sweated through the assessment and palpable relief showed on their faces when they submitted it. Marked concern wore on mine by the time I returned home, but I refused to show it the next day. We all just took one day at a time.

A great teacher levels the field for her or his students. But I refused, at least in the traditional sense. I refused to lower the expectations for my students. A great teacher doesn't level the field by lowering the expectations. A great teacher levels the field by pushing each student to his or her potential. Leveling the field doesn't mean that everyone gets to play the same amount or win the same number of games; it means you get the opportunity to become the best version of yourself.

The assessment helped me know what I already knew—I had to meet them where they were—and I liked it. I leveled the field by giving them work they could do, stretching them, encouraging them, and pushing them to do more. But I also worked *with* them. I sat with them, alongside them, coached, and did work myself. On the day of that first assessment I realized the kids were all on different planes of understanding math, but they had one common level of understanding—love. If I cared about them and what was important to them first, then they worked harder.

A Voracious Observer

As I transition into this idea of observation and quick action being a critical component to teacher and student success, I want to flashback to one incident that took place while I was a substitute at Bailey Middle School that gave me confidence *before* I went to Jere Baxter Alternative. It started with a student who had a fidgeting problem. He tapped and moved and drummed and rattled incessantly. One day, he was tapping that pencil and moving that head, humming, and working my nerves. I finally took the pencil from him. I was done—through. I wrapped it in a pipe cleaner and handed it back, so he could keep banging on the desk, but nobody else would be bothered.

No big deal, right? Wrong. I have gawked while many teachers melted down over much smaller incidents. I have watched teachers pound their heads against the wall for how their classroom is behaving, and then walk right back in and do the same thing that prompted the misbehavior over and over and over again. It's not the tapping pencil that drives the teacher or the students crazy—it's all the other expectations and unmet needs culminating in one moment with one kid who just . . . can't . . . stop . . . tapping the desk. I tried to diffuse the tension and meet the needs before they culminated in an eruption. Somehow, I missed some of my own needs: my need for peace, my need for assurance, my need for quiet confidence, but I nurtured my desire for constant distraction. A mental disruption would soon end my classroom teaching.

However, that day with the little drummer boy in my class reinforced my confidence in my ability to observe and respond. I needed that confidence in order to make it for the long haul at Jere Baxter Alternative. One more note, since I took the time to know the kid and not just identify the behavior, I handled the situation correctly. That boy was a drum major.

Now that one incident gave me the confidence I needed to observe and respond once I got to Jere Baxter Alternative. Not only was leveling the playing field a vital component to my role as a teacher, but so was observing the students and responding appropriately. Some days we worked like crazy in class. Some days, rare days, we didn't work at all. Maybe we should have. Maybe when one of the students in our class had been gunned down the night before, we should have pulled up our pants, tightened our boot straps, and pressed on. I could have made them; they would have done it for me, but who needed math when you could already count to five—the same number of bullet holes in your friend's chest? Those days we colored, and talked, and mourned.

Other days we climbed mountains. We attacked our environment socially, emotionally, and academically. For instance, we had a swearing problem. I made a swear jar. We didn't use those words in our class. In another class, we struggled with fractions, so I created a lesson where we made pancakes. We measured in fractions, divided the ingredients, and then divided the product when we were done cooking. The product is the result of multiplication. The ingredients were multiplied to feed the entire class, and the product was divided. We had full brains and stomachs on those days.

Perpendicular, bisector, and radian, oh my! Geometric ideas and terms were overwhelming, so we used string. We would attach strings to desks and tables and measure the angles. We would physically touch the string and associate the terms—high non-verbal IQs remember? After the measuring, stretching, recalculating, and discussing, the students understood the terms. If one forgot, another just had to pretend he was stretching the string.

They liked lyrics. Chants and rhymes stuck in their minds like gum in hair—you would have to cut it out. When we worked division, we would chant. You've heard of choral reading; this was choral dividing. We would chant, "Divide, multiply, subtract, bring down! Divide, multiply, subtract, bring down! Divide, multiply, subtract, bring down!" until their heads were moving, bodies were rocking, and hands were following. On test days, I would see those chairs rocking, heads moving, hands working, and I could hear them chanting, "Divide, multiply, subtract, bring down!"

Now these boys, some of them were all about the money. So, I would pay them. At first, I paid them—some of them $5.00 to turn in their homework. However, instead of giving them a raise over time, I deducted their pay. We went from $5.00 to $1.00, to candy, to an expectation. I deducted their pay, but I raised their value. When they started believing they could do it, and feeling good about their accomplishments, the reward was in the work—and their worth.

But due to a lack of love or personal education, they didn't know how to articulate their thoughts and feelings without "coming at people." We learned how to have discussions and debates without attacking one another but attacking the issue. So we did just that. We debated over Tupac and Biggie. I separated them by choice into four corners: Tupac, Biggie, On the Fence, and Persuade Me. And we debated, but we would only attack the other person's stance, not his statement or his person. The conversations were raw, the kids were real, and the topics were relevant.

Then they became interested in what I was doing. We would have silent reading time to develop reading stamina. While they read, I would read my own book. I read the novel *The Coldest Winter Ever* and the boys wanted to know what I was reading so much they couldn't stay silent. Finally, they broke the silence. "What you readin', Walk? Read that to us!"

For thirty minutes, I would have twenty-five boys—boys from the ghetto and projects, boys who didn't know their fathers and who didn't have respect for authority, boys whom everybody else had already given up on—sitting in silence and listening to me read. The boys wanted to come to class. After they promoted out of my class, they would stop by and ask to come back. We had high expectations for one another, and they loved it.

A Voracious Relative

Not only did I observe, but I could relate. Nowadays, so much media hype surrounds inappropriate student-teacher relationships that one has to be incredibly careful. Then, before the advent of social media access via smart phones, thereby before the ubiquitous access to covert means of conversation between students and teachers and the ability to instantaneously tell sensationalized stories and have them spread quickly, I had a little more flexibility, but not much. I needed to be close, but not too close. I knew the kids wouldn't respect me if they thought of me as a friend or a sister, but I could sure pull off the crazy aunt. So that's what I did. I was "crazy interested" in what they wanted to show me, but "crazy charismatic" enough to always keep them guessing. Kids respect a teacher who is a little on edge, dang near crazy, and kids, even though they may make fun of her, still invite their crazy aunt in.

In order to further the students' knowledge of geometry, I had the kids create apartments. One of the students, we'll call him T, made a mock fish aquarium with an open ceiling for easy access to the fish. When he finished his production, he proudly brought me over to elicit my approval and showed me all the multi-colored types of fish and John Deere-colored green plant life he crafted in the tank. He must have modeled twenty different types of fish in there, but he left some odd, brown blob floating at the top of the tank. I gave him a perplexed look and asked, "T, what's floating at the top of your tank?"

He leaned forward excitedly over the tank, a sly smile coyly flashing across his face, "Oh, c'mon, Walk, you know what that is! You know there is always a dead roach floating at the top of the tank!"

I could relate. In fact, that is one of the reasons the boys respected me so much: I understood their jokes and their hardships. As I teach in my seminars covering special education, or in my classroom at Belmont University, or in the abuse prevention and counseling group, "We all spell struggle the same way," and for these boys, my

experience with their personal struggles in my own life made me relative—a relative. Not only could I relate to their passion and pain, but I
had seen things they had not seen. I had survived L.A: "Respect!"

The nature of an alternative school encourages students to be transient. They come and hopefully go back to their original campus, and I
hustled and strived to make a difference while they were with me. One
imperative was to maintain a high level of respect from my students. I
earned it, and when new students came into the class, they knew it.

Discussions of gang activity and gang affiliation permeated the walls
of the classrooms, restrooms, and lunchroom daily. In a gang, loyalty
rules, and my students understood that code. In my room, respect required loyalty, and we indoctrinated the new students very quickly. I
don't condone or promote gang activity, but in my room, I was the
"Original Gansta'." In their minds, I represented "the land." I grew up
in L.A., so I knew the lingo, the signs, the drama. Respect embodied a
prized commodity for these students, as did loyalty, and I earned both.

One student decided to test it. I enforced a rule that students may not
keep their phone on their person during class. When I saw it, I gave a
warning, a polite reminder. If it happened again, I took the phone until
the end of the day. This particular day, a student I'll call Alfred started
playing on his phone. I asked him to put the phone away. He yanked
the phone back out only a few moments later, so I had him hand it
over, and I crammed it in my desk. I could feel his tension rising, I
could see him staring at me, I knew he planned to act, but before I
could diffuse the situation, he moved.

He rushed the desk and started screaming, "Give me my fucking
phone! Give me my fucking phone!" I didn't. He kept cursing me and
calling me names and trying to reach into the desk. He started to
threaten me, and the other kids went crazy.

Chair legs shrieked against the floor as kids stood up. The volume of
raised voices and movement pushed the atmosphere to the front of the
room. I slipped in between him and the other students. White eyeballs
and gaping mouths pressed forward, followed by flailing arms and
brightly colored clothes. A shot rang out! It was the clack of my heel
on the floor when I stomped my foot. On one side I had a student
threatening me, and on the other side I had a group of boys lurching
forward to get at him. They pressed in. He continued cussing me, running his mouth like diarrhea, and I turned to him and said, "You better
stop talkin' cause these boys are trying to give you the business!"

With his mouth still running, I spoke commandingly, moved briskly,
and utilized proximity control to calm the students, which diffused the

situation and kept Alfred protected. Talk about loving your enemies. As soon as the student resource officer escorted Alfred from the room, the boys complained, "Walk, you should have let us jump him. He disrespected you, Walk! You should have let us jump him."

You have never smelled "stank" like the smell of twenty boys whose aggression peaked at the same time in one small space. "Stanky!" understates the toxic smell in the room after that incident, but the smell was worth it considering the lessons I learned. My students loved me, and I loved enough to protect someone, to stand up for what was right, even when he had done something wrong.

We protect the ones we love. In some situations we loan, and in others we give. For a time, I was giving certain students twenty dollars a week if they attended class each day. I taught one student who was very emphatic about being there daily. Mr. Ragamuffin, as I'll call him, never missed a day. Attending school didn't create a problem for him, keeping his clothes on did. Every day he would keep taking his shoes off. I'd say, "Mr. Ragamuffin, I need you to put your shoes back on," and he would. Later on in the period he would be buffing the floor with his socked feet while his shoes sat upright underneath his chair.

I confronted the situation, looking at him with deep concern.

"What's going on with your shoes? Why do you take them off all the time?"

"Walk, these shoes are too small. They're not even my shoes; they're my brother's."

"Now, why are you wearing your brother's shoes?"

"Well, they're my little brother's. I let my older brother borrow my shoes, and he was wearing them when he got arrested."

"Oh! So the shoes went with your brother and the police?"

That conversation bothered me all weekend long. I kept thinking about it, praying about it. The next week I began asking him about shoes.

"So, Mr. R, if you were ballin' in the NBA right now, and you didn't have your own shoe line, whose shoes would you be rockin'?"

"Walk, you know I'd be rockin' those new Kobes! C'mon, Walk, erebody loves those shoes!"

The next weekend I bought those shoes. I pulled him into the office, and I said, "You can't tell anybody about this. You know I can't do this for everybody, but I bought you these shoes." He came back to school the following day, wearing those shoes so conspicuously that even the sidewalk noticed. He showed them off, *flossing* as they used to say, but kept it low key about how he got them—from his uncle!

Finally, some female students enrolled in my classes, and their arrival punctured the once rough-and-tumble and nonchalant attitudes of the boys, especially concerning appearance. Wearing nice shoes drew attention, but with girls in the classroom, attention to detail stretched beyond shoes—way beyond. Clothes matter at an alternative school. Maybe even more than at a traditional school because the clothes say something about who you are and where you're from, even if you have to wear a uniform. My female students created ways to make their uniforms distinct and unique, from tying their shirts, rolling their pants, wearing slim-fitting or loose-fitting combos, colored undershirts, and myriad accessories—oh the accessories! Have mercy!

However, one of the girls arrived in class shockingly wrinkled from the floor up. Her pants were wrinkled, her shirt was wrinkled, her hair was mussed. I wouldn't have been surprised if her socks were wrinkled. Compassion leaked from my pores when I caught the self-conscious and defensive expression written on her face. I pulled her aside.

"Are the lights off?"

"No, ma'am."

My compassion waned slightly. *Then why are you so mussed?* I wondered.

"Do you have an iron?"

"No, ma'am."

She dropped her head down and rolled her eyes away, nearly squinting.

"I'm sorry, baby. I'm going to get you an iron, but when I do, don't you come to school all wrinkled again, you hear?" She was smiling now.

"Yes, ma'am!"

I brought the iron the next day. Clothes mattered to them, but the self-respect represented by taking care of themselves mattered all the more.

Not only did the students crave the attention of their classmates, but they wanted more of me. The kids wanted time. Oh my goodness, they wanted time! I drove to their houses after school, staying late, to conduct what could truly be called extended tutorials. Some incidents manufactured awkward experiences. I rolled with the punches. More often than I can remember, a roach would come crawling up the couch or table and I would say, "Hand me that shoe so I can kill this roach!"

I would exterminate the roaches with the shoe, and we would keep on working as if nothing happened. I acted like the incident was insignificant though I could feel the student's' embarrassment. Again, I could relate.

Parents appreciated my concern and unorthodox tactics. The crazy aunt gets to have all the fun. As a reward for academic or behavioral achievement, I further motivated specific students by taking them to breakfast. I would drive to their house, talk to their parents, explain I didn't want anything—I didn't touch little boys—then take the boys to a favorite restaurant. I explained explicitly that the meal was a reward for achievement, not because I had an inappropriate interest in the boys. I had to make that clear. We would go eat breakfast and the boys would tell me what was really important to them—spill the beans so to speak. They knew they could trust me, and trust made all the difference.

Before I left Jere Baxter Alternative school, I made one very significant home visit I am sure made an impression. One of my most talented students decided he wasn't going to finish his final exam. He didn't like to appear smart or to be singled out, even by success. After school, I drove to his house and parked out front. He was joshing on the stoop with some of his friends when he saw me coming. He rolled his eyes and dropped his head as I marched up there in my dress and heels, paper in hand. Right there in front of his friends, I said, "Oh no. We're not going to leave this test half-finished. We are going to march right in there to the table and finish this exam." And we did.

I thoroughly enjoyed my time at Jere Baxter Alternative, and I learned so much. I learned about teaching and life and patience. I learned more about prayer and more about loss. Most importantly, I learned to pay attention to my students. I learned my students. I didn't always learn everything I needed in school, but at Jere Baxter Alternative, I learned about my students. I left the school to join the Navy in the summer of 2006. I wish I had taken a little more time to learn about myself.

A Voracious Redeemer

"For my power is made perfect in weakness." 2 Corinthians 12:9

Dressing nice and looking well were always a priority. As was uniformity. In middle school, I had joined the Cadets, and I performed in color guard. I liked to march and keep rhythm. I liked sequence, cadence, and uniformity. After two successful years teaching at Jere Baxter Alternative, I chose to join the Navy. (Enter the force working against me—the self-sabotage.) Can you see it? Can you see the alien abductor? My childhood dreams were of teaching, curricula, and school, but my priorities hinged on how I looked. I interrupted my dreams by joining the Navy. I am proud of my attempt to serve, but it was a disruption, a straying point, a chaotic mind-field I had created. You see, I excelled as a teacher, but the anxiety wore off, and I needed more. Peace in life led to war in me.

In 2006, I was in the Delayed Entry program. Tensions arose in me. Service, protection, and leadership drove me. The chaos in my childhood had slowly numbed in adulthood stability, and the military battle called.

Officer Candidate School (OCS) is an educational and military opportunity allowing college graduates to bypass standard boot camp in favor of attending OCS and entering the military as an officer. I took the test to enter OCS, but I did not fare well. Angry, my heart kept pushing me forward. I had to serve. After my abysmal performance on the entrance exam, I heard military personnel state that entering the military through boot camp like everyone else created the only certain pathway to respect. Some people had a bad taste for those who entered through OCS.

I arrived in Grand Rapids, Chicago, for boot camp on June 6, 2006. Several years older than most cadets, I was eager and experienced, so I leapfrogged into a chief yeoman's position. My maturity—I was twenty-nine years old working with adult children of eighteen to twenty years old—earned me a leadership position. Life had prepared me well, and I exuded military professionalism.

But my heart was broken. My brother had died the year before, and I had never dealt with the childhood abuse, the abandonment, the transient upbringing, the homelessness—none of it. My own body conspired against my mind and brought everything to a crashing halt.

Throughout boot camp, I still performed well, but my broken past led me to seek out counseling. Apathy wasn't the culprit luring me away, neither was depression shackling my aspirations; I was injured, unhealed, broken. The pain wouldn't subside. Being in top physical condition didn't change the malnutrition of my heart. Leading groups of cadets and having the respect of my peers and superiors didn't mend my soul. Achievement doesn't knit back together a torn soul; it only puts more frays in the fabric.

The counselor helped me see I was creating chaos around me to supplement for the chaos removed by my hard work. Let me say it another way, my hard work in the classroom had created a stable environment for my students and me. The financial stability, relational stability, and respect I earned had frightened me. I loathed the peace. The counselor had me reevaluate my decision to join the Navy. She had me leave.

Although I left the Navy shortly after joining, I did nearly complete boot camp, but I had to return to fight a war of my own against an enemy I couldn't see, one who worked harder the harder I worked. I knew, then, I had better learn how to fight quickly, or else it would be too late.

A Voracious Teacher

I was still reeling when I returned from the Navy. I understood I had substituted work chaos and achievement for the rejection and chaos of my early life. I knew I belonged in teaching, so I enrolled in a master's program at David Lipscomb University and I was awarded a teaching position at Hillsboro High School. I began learning my lesson. I had found little solace in peace, and I craved the noise, the friction.

When I started at Hillsboro High School, there was none of that. Hillsboro was a different place, much more calm and docile, but the challenge was that it was new—my new distraction.

Don't misunderstand: I loved teaching and I would never trade that time I had with my students. Teaching did not serve as a distraction; I truly believe I was made for it, and it came naturally for that very reason. However, I do wish I had paid attention—I wish I had paid attention to my pain. Instead, I submerged the pain in my work and in my purpose.

Hillsboro High School is in a small suburb of Nashville that is very affluent and has a diverse population. Unlike the alternative school, which was diverse racially, Hillsboro was diverse culturally. Although the school was composed of predominately white students, a multitude of students of different ethnicities, faiths, and races attended. There were Irish and Polish students, Jewish and Bahái faith students, Muslim and Hindi students, as well as many teenagers hailing from Africa, Asia, the Middle East, and so on.

Within the school, another level of diversity existed, and it was the diverse learners. Years ago, these would have been the students in the LD (Learning Disabled) classes. Now, we realize the label doesn't make the student. The student may have had some special needs, and that is where I came in. I was there to meet those special needs.

All of my students had IEPs (Individualized Education Program), but I taught them and treated them as if they were students in a general education class. I met their IEPs, but more significantly, I made sure to meet them where they were and push them forward.

My teaching style helped the students work to the level of the general-education curriculum, to exceed even their own expectations. Most didn't have any physical impairments or external indications that learning was difficult for them—they were not socially awkward nor did they struggle to hold a conversation—but they did have significant learning disabilities: short-term memory loss, delayed processing, comprehension deficits, cognitive impairments. For these kids, school can be especially tough because it seems that nobody sees it—you can't see what's on the inside. They look and act "normal," but school is a serious struggle, and we all feel and spell struggle the same way.

They loved to learn. Their parents stayed involved, unlike the alternative school, but just like the alternative school, I helped the students learn by giving them a point of reference. For that very reason, I loved to teach the ecosystem. When I peeked into their lives by asking about their neighborhoods and homes, my students became fountains of information, gushing with details. I listened intently, and then I would drive through their neighborhood searching for connections. Once I had a point of reference—like Tupac and Biggie at the alternative school—I could bring the functions of the ecosystem home to the students. Then, I could make the connection to a whale or turtle or spider monkey. Although I was incredibly successful in that teaching role, old prejudices lingered.

A monkey still rode my back at Hillsboro, but it was just a different type of monkey than I experienced at my previous teaching position. At Jere Baxter Alternative, I was normal—the monkey was self-imposed. I was just an African-American teacher from L.A. with a *sick* work ethic. At Hillsboro, I was abnormal—the monkey was culturally imposed. Although we had a very diverse staff, something about being a young, black female educator in a white neighborhood aroused a certain air of suspicion. Maybe it was just my insecurities.

On the night of parent-teacher conferences, I understood. I watched a parent come in the door and I greeted her in the hallway entrance. This parent shook my hand, sized me up, and decided I must be support staff, a helper, a paraprofessional, but not a teacher. She started gushing about how she wanted to meet Ms. Walker, how her daughter loved Ms. Walker, and how she wanted to thank Ms. Walker. When she finished, I politely said, "I'm Ms. Walker!" I could tell she was shocked. Maybe it was my race, maybe it was my appearance, maybe it was my speaking style. She was shocked to find out I was Ms. Walker.

I was proud to be Ms. Walker. I was proud because my students grew academically and personally. At that time, a student had to pass the Gateway Exam to graduate. The hurdle: I taught students with special learning needs. Some of them had scored a 14 on the exam the year prior, and they needed a 22 to pass. After one year of teaching them through projects, activities, hands-on experiences, common sense, and complex activities, I had one student jump from a score of 14 to a score of 42. Students began to double and triple their scores from the previous year, so I was proud to be Ms. Walker. But at the same time, I just wasn't proud to be Shree.

One final memory I have before I left Hillsboro High School is of a boy whom I will call Melvin. Those days, I had my hair really short. Melvin found an opportunity to give me a hard time about it. Just after Valentine's Day he stopped by my classroom, interrupted the class, and yelled, "Hey, Walk, I got you something!"

Sighing, I turned to him and said, "What do you have for me?"

He held up a stuffed monkey holding a heart, and said, "Happy Valentine's Day! I got you this monkey because you two have the same haircut!"

The class exploded with laughter, and after failed attempts to suppress it, I looked at him as if to say, *Hand me that stupid monkey, you smart* . . . Although I pretended to be perturbed, I found it sweet. Prank or not, my students were even thinking about me around Valentine's Day.

A Voracious Warrior

I returned to Jere Baxter Alternative to teach in 2008. I kept leaning forward, leaning into teaching, leaning into my career. I had finished my master's at David Lipscomb University in December of 2007, but I still hadn't finished my teaching licensure. I had not secured it, so I was insecure. Getting by on talent, grit, and determination worked well, but now I started to become anxious about my job. Then my test-taking anxiety awoke from its slumber.

I taught test-taking strategies to my students, but I had never used them in the past. Now, the time came for me to practice what I preached, and I was scared. The Praxis test was intimidating, the horror stories were nightmarish. Practice became my friend. I developed a time-management strategy and studied the practice tests. I timed myself over and over on the practice tests, studied the questions to determine how the test makers arrived at the answers, and read, and read, and read. The preparation was exhausting, but I passed on the first try. Goodbye, anxiety.

Now, with a secured licensure, I worked a job I loved, I framed and hung my master's degree, I portended upward mobility, I felt peace, and I had this nagging feeling that there should be something more happening. Something bad. Something chaotic. And there was—a battle for my soul.

At the end of my time at Jere Baxter Alternative, I discovered I couldn't be content in contentment. My body craved chaos. I couldn't find peace in peace. I felt like I was scratching my head, but it didn't itch. I was scratching for no reason other than I wanted it to itch. And the scratching was addictive. I couldn't stop scratching.

My experience in the Navy should have been my first clue, but I overlooked it and jumped back into the challenge of teaching in a new place and seeking another degree. My discussions with the counselor should have been a clue. My never-tiring desire to improve should have been a clue. Learning from my students' behavior should have been a clue. But I didn't have a clue.

I leaned further forward. I soon got promoted to a new position at Jere Baxter Middle School where I began coordinating six sites for Twilight school. I taught at Jere Baxer Alternative by day and held the new administrative position over Twilight school at Jere Baxter Middle by night. Twilight school served as an alternative to students getting Out of School Suspension (OSS) and losing their seat hours in the classroom. The students could attend Twilight school, make up the hours, and not get charged with OSS. I managed the scheduling of the six sites as well as the scheduling at my middle school. I continually received positive reports about my work ethic, flexibility, and most often, my efficiency. I felt like I was in a place of prominence, but my brokenness began to leak out.

During a scheduled meeting at Jere Baxter Alternative, I broke down crying. I wasn't sure why I was crying, and I couldn't control it. My pulse increased, my eyes looked down, my thinking slowed, my mind clouded. I wanted to disappear, but I was conducting the meeting. The tears kept coming, but I had no reason to cry. Drop after drop after drop fell from my cheeks, some on my blouse, some on my crossed forearms, and some on the table. Surely, the people in the room thought I was crazy. I still marched on with the meeting while my body knew what my heart couldn't conceive.

I was depressed, and I was broken, and I couldn't work my way out of it. Actually, the more I struggled for significance, the deeper I dug the hole. I tried to tuck myself inside myself to disappear, but the problem reigned inside me.

I went to a therapist and she diagnosed me with Seasonal Affective Disorder (SAD). The knowledge didn't change me. I kept searching. I bought a light box, a flat-paned lamp that emits light mimicking the effect of sunlight as a means of therapy for SAD, and it helped, but it didn't change me. I continued to see my therapist, and it helped, but it didn't change me. I couldn't change. I was like a broken mirror: seven years of bad luck and someone better throw me out and buy a new one before getting cut.

I existed in a dark room, with no way to get out. I felt more than sad, I felt stuck, alone, surrounded. One weekend, I left work and went straight to my therapist. She always worked me into her schedule, always—but not this time. On this Friday, she couldn't. We spoke briefly, but I had to leave on my own. Alone. I left my phone at school. I didn't need to call anybody. My mind was made up. Nobody needed to know. I was bringing this misery to an end.

I drove to my apartment, nearly crawled to the front door, trudged back to my bedroom, opened up my top dresser drawer, and pulled it out. Hesitancy and fear surrounded me, my pulse racing. My sweat and tears created troughs down my cheeks. Silence filled the room. I knew what I had to do. I wanted this so badly, I wanted the pain to end, but fear choked me. I set my face firmly, rolled my finger inside the tab, stared down, leaned my head back, and cried out. I laid the Bible open on the ground before me, and I poured my heart out to God. I prayed violently. I wept. I screamed. I wrestled. I lost it.

I lost the expectations I had placed on myself. I lost the belief my worth came from what other people thought of me. I lost the feeling I had done something wrong, that it was my fault I had been abused, molested, raped. I lost the notion that the words of others could fill my heart or accolades could fill my soul. I lost my life.

I committed suicide that night. I killed the life planted in the belief that accomplishment made me whole and acceptance gave me worth. I found my worth in who God said I am. His child. My whole life had been burdened with trying to earn back what I had lost, to achieve what I desired, to become, in someone else's eyes, significant. But I only felt whole when I gave that up.

Jesus said something interesting about our lives. He said, "For whoever would save his life will lose it, but whoever loses his life for my sake will find it" (Matthew 16:25). I am not sure everything He meant by His statement, but I know I found more purpose in giving my pain to God than I did in trying to save my life by my hands.

The enemy I couldn't see was in me, telling me I am not enough, pushing me, creating chaos, looking for noise and friction, hating peace. I finally started to fight back, and I started by handing the battle over to the Prince of Peace, the Mighty Warrior. The warning signs had been flashing all along. I had spent so much time learning: learning my environment, learning how to survive, learning in my classes, learning about my students—and I had neglected to learn about myself.

I was a mirage, a glass bottle filled with a beautiful ship, sails raised full-mast, appearing as if the glass were formed around the fully erected ship. The truth is, I had striven for the appearance of a ship in full sail inside the bottle, but I didn't know how to achieve it. I didn't know the Master Builder constructed the ship outside of the bottle, placed it inside, and hoisted the sails within when He saw fit. When I died to the mirage, I learned who I was by learning more about who had built me. I wasn't ready to have my sails raised just yet, because an enemy, an alien, had come in and clipped a few strings. My Builder wanted to repair me before He put me on display.

I went back to work on Monday a remade person. I repented of my old beliefs, and I began to trust that God loved me as His child. I became *wise* when I accepted the psalm's proclamation: "I am fearfully and wonderfully made" (Psalm 139:14) and God's declaration that I was "very good" (Genesis 1:31). From 2008 through 2017, I was promoted three times within Metro Nashville Public schools, but not for prestige, but because I was being prepared. I also began and completed an Educational Specialist and doctoral program at Tennessee State University, not for accolades, but because I wanted to help those in need.

Christ knew me. He *learned* me—much better than I ever could have learned my students—as He did the prophet Jeremiah, "Before I formed you in the womb I knew you" (Jeremiah 1:5), and He *leveled* the places before me: "I will go before you and level the exalted places" (Isaiah 45:2). When I trust Him, I am a great learner and leveler. I learned peace does not come from a set of circumstances, and it doesn't arrive when we do. Peace comes with trust.

Another enemy exists I cannot see. I hear he walks around, prowling, looking for helpless victims he can consume. I read he asked to sift one guy like wheat and wreak havoc on another man and all his family. I've heard that he tempts people in their weakest moments by their greatest need, food for the hungry, identity for the unimportant, security for the insecure. I've never seen him, but I believe he was the one who taught me not to trust. Some say he is a conspiracy, a theory contrived by fear and lunacy. Jesus didn't think so. This enemy loves chaos, and he sent sick men into my bedroom late at night and into my weakness at inopportune times. I am fighting him now, fighting back, but in the past, he taught me never to trust.

Relationships

Turst

"After a certain point, a heart with so many stress fractures would never be anything but broken."
–Jodi Picoult, *Salem Falls*

My earliest memory of my father was when we lived in the projects, and he came to pick me up on his motorcycle. He and my mother had split, again, and he drove over to visit me. I remember his picking me up and placing me on the back of the motorcycle, right behind him. He warned me, "Hold on tight," before he started the bike. I did. I held on with every ounce of energy my little body could muster. I felt the wind whip around his body, off his back, and against my face. I inhaled his scent and hung on to my daddy.

We rode to the park, and once we arrived, we opened our coloring books and crayons. We sat on the bench and we lay on the grass, and we colored pictures. The experience felt like it lasted for hours, but it also seemed brief, like it lasted only a few hurried seconds, and then it was gone. He brought me back home, dropped me off with my mother, started his bike again, and rode off to his other life—the one without me.

My father, Connie, grew up in Carson, California, on the right side of the tracks. His home spanned nearly three thousand square feet, in California, in the 1970s. My father was raised upper-middle class. He had an arcade in his home, trophies on the walls, and two parents at the dinner table. Well, his mother had earned the trophies on the wall. She was a great bowler, and she won so many bowling trophies with ease she expected to be a winner and to be prized.

On the other hand, my mother grew up without trophies. Trophies didn't serve a purpose in their home. What did they have to celebrate? What type of trophies do you put up for a lifetime of non-achievement? These are the types of questions one begins to ask when she looks at the differences between the affluent and the deprived, the wealthy and the poverty-stricken, the rich and the poor, my father and my mother.

Since Momma grew up on the wrong side of the tracks, and Daddy grew up on the right side, Momma was never fully received by Daddy's family. She was just a girl from the wrong side of the tracks, and I was just a result of when a boy from the right side hooks up with a girl from the wrong side. They were only fifteen when I was born, and by the time they celebrated each other's nineteenth birthdays, they had brought three children into the world together. Three children, on the wrong side of the tracks.

Deceit shadows a man who produces three children by the time he is nineteen but cannot give his own daughter a compliment. Clearly, if a boy of fourteen can sleep with a girl of the same age, he knows how to give a compliment. If he can repeat the cycle, in spite of his parents' objections, but never has to take full responsibility for his children, he must *really* know how to dole out compliments. If he manages to maintain a few other relationships on the side, sleeping with all of those women too, he has demonstrated that he can "work his game" with the best of them. He's a sweet talker, so he wears a mask because he's really a con man if he can only give a compliment to get what he wants, but he can't bring himself to give one for the benefit of his own daughter.

I love my father. He was appropriately named *Con*nie, and he is where my trust breaks down. I am his oldest child, his first daughter, his baby girl, but I was from the wrong side of the tracks. He made me believe I was special by calling me "Princess," but he just couldn't play the prince when I needed it.

Daddy would *con*vince himself he was being a good father by inconsistently doing a few good things. He would stop in and see us. He would buy us presents. One time he even came by to take me shopping for new school clothes. Since his child support and involvement in our lives had been inconsistent, I guess he felt like this was a way to take responsibility and make up for some of his failures. We spent the entire day shopping, and he spent more than two thousand dollars on me. On just me. Being splurged on felt so wonderful, but it morphed into guilt. Daddy never came back to take Connie or Iesheia, my two younger siblings, school shopping. His behavior was inconsistent, immature. Another time, he splurged on presents for all of us, including my stepsiblings Momma had after she and Daddy finally split: Daron and Otis. If you're reading this and thinking, *That guy can't win for losing*, you're missing the picture. I respect my father for all those times he took responsibility and was loving and giving, even when he didn't have to be. What hurts is that his love shone on his terms, not when I needed it. I knew Daddy loved me. But he always reserved himself for himself.

He grew another family, and I didn't fit into that one. I understood, so I didn't try to. They didn't know much about me and neither did most of his friends. To this day, if I visit him in California, he will introduce me to people and they obviously don't know I exist. I am a misshapen puzzle piece, a stowed-away chip from a past game, a secret.

My first memory of really needing my father was just days after I confessed to being molested. Momma knew about the molestation; I told her about what happened to me, and she let me go see Daddy for a few days while she sorted things out. I wasn't just shipped off to my father's to get me out the way. Momma pushed much deeper than that. She had taken me to the doctor and scheduled appointments and tried to set up some counseling, but then thought it may do me some good to get away.

I went to see my dad and his new girlfriend, Charlotte. I remember I had on a two-piece jacket and an A-line puffy skirt. The skirt had black and green stripes, and I was wearing matching bangle bracelets. My hair was braided to the side, and I felt so pretty. My heart cried out for validation. I twirled around and cocked my head to the side and smiled my toothy grin. I don't remember if I was missing baby teeth at the time, but I imagine I was, swinging my little torso side to side, smiling. I would get in his way and think, *Just tell me I'm enough.* He didn't. Just one compliment, that was all I was asking. It never came. Daddy never complimented me that weekend, or hugged me, but he did make fun of me for not knowing how to spell "federal" on *Wheel of Fortune*. I can spell it now. I can spell "federal" and "struggle" and "dysfunctional" all the same as everyone else. I just can't spell "turst."

I love my dad. I really do. I have tried to honor his opinions and his privacy throughout my life, and I still do. I often wonder who had broken his heart to make him act the way he did Now, I see that some of the games he played with us and with our minds were the same games he played with his own. I heard once, "We lie to no one so well as we lie to ourselves," and I believe this is true. I hope my dad escapes from behind that lie, but for now, I have chosen to love him from a distance, the only way he has ever let me.

Building Trust

"She was just another broken doll dreaming of a boy with glue."
–Atticus

In 1994, a local high school had an elite running back (whom I'll call No Name). But I knew his name. At the time I attended Fremont High School, was an athletic trainer for the football team, and worked on the school paper. The other school, where the boy with the pretty face and no name played, was one of our rivals. As one of the trainers for the football team, I kept myself entrenched with my school's football players and their success. The other school wasn't a big concern; they couldn't beat anybody, but nobody could stop the running back with no name—not even me. Maybe, I didn't want to.

While I was working as a trainer for the football team and writing for the school newspaper and pursuing various extracurricular interests, I also had a boyfriend. His name was Zeus, and he was a looker. Zeus was a young, clean-cut, polished, Mexican boy with penetrating brown eyes and a wicked smile that could melt glass. He smiled and laughed a lot, which made him attractive and fun. His brother, however, didn't smile much at all when I was around. I was the wrong color and didn't speak the right language for Zeus' *hermano*.

During a game against our rival, No Name had come to the game to watch both teams, but instead noticed me and talked about me, unbridled, to his friends. His friend baited him to come talk to me, which No Name didn't do reluctantly. The thing is: I rejected him. Zeus was my boyfriend, and I didn't need the drama, so I rejected No Name. But Zeus found out about it anyway.

Diving into the logic of a high school boy is like falling in a bottomless pit: you'll never hit anything solid. The logic seems . . . nonexistent. No Name was popular, very popular. He was being scouted by USC, UCLA, Nebraska, and several other schools. Some say a recruiter from Notre Dame visited him because No Name had mentioned Lou Holtz. Everyone knew No Name, and when Zeus found out that No Name had talked to me, it created jealousy.

In Zeus' mind, rejecting No Name was not enough, I should have never spoken with him publicly—that was disrespectful. (As if speaking with him privately would have been more respectful.) Zeus was intimidated and insecure, and he broke up with me only to fall quickly into the loving arms of an awaiting freshman girl. He paraded her around the school and was desperately affectionate with her, which made me jealous. He had never acted that way with me. His actions confirmed what I already believed: *I was not enough.*

But No Name was different, he validated me. He pursued me. He showed me I was enough.

No Name, No Shame

When a car rolls up next to you corner of 76th and Broadway, your first question isn't "I wonder who they're here to help?" At least mine wasn't. That is definitely not what I thought when that gold Ford Tempo came bouncing into the corner lot. I was walking home from school as the wind whipped down the street and blew the dust up in fountains of hazy fumes. My thoughts were my own until the gold fender of the car shot right across my path, teeming with boys. I hesitated. Normally, there would be a catcall, an inappropriate comment, or an invitation to join them in the car. This day was different. When the front passenger door opened, out stepped No Name, and he looked directly at me, through those light eyes that dropped into his chiseled face. He pretended for a second to compute recognition, then surprise, but obviously he had seen me as the car bounded down the street. He saw me.

No Name introduced himself the way that young boys do at the corner store, with a look, a smile, and then words. We spoke. We hustled through the pleasantries, made small talk, and I told him about how he had caused me to lose my boyfriend. He leaned forward and looked into my eyes, "Do you have a boyfriend now?"

I smiled, acting coy, "No." He asked, now smiling, if he could have my number, which I, now deadpanned and staring up intensely at him, gave to him.

We continued to talk; I could feel this was different. This wasn't just some boy pursuing me for my body. He looked at me and talked to me like I was a person, like I mattered, like I was real.

I started to relax and let the front fall . . . I don't remember if No Name took down my number on paper or if he just memorized it, but he had my number, and time would tell if what I thought about him was true—I really couldn't stop him, he wouldn't give up until he got what he wanted. He wanted me to be his girl. The moment I felt he was about to leave, that his body and smiling face were going to pull away, I started to reel myself back in emotionally. I had been slightly too convinced, a little too forward, and I didn't want him to know I was *that* interested.

The wind had other plans. Down the cross street the wind fluttered and blew against us, facing each other. At just the wrong time, I turned ever so slightly, and the wind caught the inside of the back of my dress, ballooning it with air, and blowing it up above my waist!

For a moment, time stood still. I looked into his eyes as I batted my dress back down with my arms to cover myself, standing cross-legged. His eyes laughed, but his mouth did not. I played it cool, but I was burning up inside. I was so embarrassed! After I began to laugh, No Name began to laugh and my peek-a-boo became a story we laughed about when we reflected back on old times. No Name always said I tried to entice him that day on the corner of 76th and Broadway. The wind had a sense of humor too, but I had the last laugh. I had put on shorts underneath my dress that morning. Shameless!

Sharing Trust

The reason I trusted No Name so quickly was his mentality clicked with my psyche. He did not approach me as a young boy, out to get his. No Name was a man. He was driven, and I could tell by his determination that I wasn't a possession—he didn't feel entitled—but I was something—someone—worth pursuing. He was driven and I was driven; we just clicked.

I still didn't feel like *enough*. I had my worries. *Was I just another notch in his belt? He's different. Am I worthy to be his girlfriend?* But our relationship blossomed. We understood each other from the soul outward, not from the outside in. No Name had experienced abandonment too. His mom had abandoned him for a while when he was a young child. He lived with his grandparents, then his aunt, and then his mom again in tenement housing. We both had trust issues with adults, with our parents, so we belonged to each other. He made me feel connected; like I belonged.

At night, No Name came to my house and stayed with me while I did my homework by candlelight. He knew school was important to me, and the lack of electricity in our home didn't seem to bother him either. He just wanted to be with me. School was important to him too. He had a 3.8 GPA in high school, even though he spent his evenings with me.

Early one morning, around 2:00 a.m., my aunt came bursting through my bedroom door. I seized with fear. "No Name's here for you," she said, then walked back to her room. The fear melted. I uncurled. That was it, nothing traumatizing had happened, nobody had died; No Name had just come over to see me—at 2:00 in the morning! We sat on the front porch and gazed wonder-eyed at the stars. We talked of everything and nothing. *I loved that boy.*

Our relationship consummated understanding. We understood lemons were meant to make lemonade. We understood compassion was a driving force for change. We understood, most importantly, we needed each other.

The school year came to a close and I was still No Name's girlfriend. We both graduated. No Name went to a prestigious university in Texas. I never got to see him play college football live in person, but I was his girlfriend. I moved to Texas for a while, didn't get to see him much, so I moved back to L.A., but I was still his girlfriend. We didn't spend the holidays together, but I was still his girlfriend. Everyone knew it. Everyone knew I was his girlfriend; even when I moved to Nashville, I was still his girlfriend. Even though he was dating some girl down there in Texas, I was still his girlfriend. I never got to see him play, I never saw him on holidays, I never had him all to myself, but I was his girlfriend! It was stupid, the whole thing was. Or maybe I was stupid.

I sometimes wonder if we are each other's unfinished business in this life. And if we die right at this moment, will our souls rest in peace knowing that we have accomplished what we came here for? Or will this be one of those lives where we pass up the chance to collide, to be more than almost, to be together, and to intertwine our souls into one?
'On next life, love,' he said.
And I cannot help but wonder if that's a lie that he's been telling me from life to life. (Cynthia Go)

Breaking Trust

"She tried to fix her broken pieces with all the things that broke her."
–Atticus

I wonder if he'll be here. I wonder if he'll be here. I wonder if he'll be here. This was a big deal for me, and I needed him to be there. I waited. I looked around the room. I put my hands up to shield my eyes from the florescent lighting and I stood on my tiptoes to try to see him. I never did. He never showed. I had invited my father to my sixth-grade graduation; he said he would come, but he never showed.

My father never came to any of my graduations. Honestly, he only showed up for what he wanted, when he wanted, on his terms. My mother wouldn't chase him down for child support, so he didn't pay. It wasn't on his terms. He told me later that he had come to my graduation, but he stood on the street corner and couldn't will himself through the door. He didn't stand on *no* street corner. No way. His body never darkened the doorway that day because he was *invited*. Showing up for the graduation wasn't his idea, so he didn't show. Momma didn't chase after him, so he didn't pay. It wasn't on his terms. I had chased after him, so he didn't show. It wasn't on his terms. Immature.

After I graduated, I had an experience with Daddy that pushed *broke* into *broken*. He had met a lady named Lawand when I was younger, whom he eventually married. Lawand had children and Daddy became their stepfather. He never had money or time for us once he got together with Lawand.

Lawand was a pleaser, not like my mother. Momma wouldn't back down ever. I remember one time when, as a child, I had an accident and peed on myself. Daddy, in his own brokenness, thought I should stand in the wet filth and stench to learn my lesson. Momma was not having it. They started screaming. They started pushing. Then Daddy blackened her eyes. Momma has had problems with her eyes ever since. Seems like Daddy won that battle, but Momma eventually outfoxed the fox.

As we grew older, and Daddy married Lawand, Momma was still in the picture. She and Daddy shared children together, and she knew he would be in and out of her life, so she always had Lawand's ear. Momma would braid hair for Lawand's kids. Where we lived, Momma could never be too sure who was her friend and who was her enemy. If anything ever happened to her, someone would have to help take care of her children, so she had Lawand's ear, which messed with Daddy, and she tried to appeal to Lawand's heart.

When I moved back from Texas, after going down there to start anew and be close to No Name, my trust in my father eroded, and my trust in No Name began to fade. Daddy made comments such as, "You know No Name is cheating on you down there, don't you? You know he's got him another girl down there, don't you?" I didn't, and I didn't stop trying to help my father either.

Lawand didn't have custody of her children at the time. The kids lived in a house with Lawand's mom, but she couldn't take care of them. I represented the solution. Arriving back from Texas, jobless, I became the live-in nanny, while Daddy and Lawand did their thing. For two months, that was the situation. Monday through Friday, I was the acting mom. I cooked and cleaned, got the kids up and off to school, did homework with them, parented them; basically, I did everything.

One Friday evening, Daddy and Lawand came over to the house. Lawand had called and asked him what he wanted for dinner and he told her a burrito. Lawand ran all around town trying to get what the kids wanted, what Daddy wanted, what everybody wanted to make everybody happy. Only, Daddy wasn't happy. He was mad. Lawand had spent all her time and money chasing rainbows to make everyone happy, and all Daddy could see was wasted time, expense, and a cold burrito. So he started a fight.

The kids played "Ring Around the Rosie" in the bedroom while Daddy and Lawand started to get loud. The kids kept playing and only got louder themselves. The window was open and the noise from the street invaded the house and crashed into the yelling inside, typhooning into a bitter shattering wind of sound. The room grew hot, breathless. Daddy and Lawand began to tussle back and forth; the kids kept playing.

I sat back as the room circled around me. Daddy hit Lawand. She hit him back. He hit her again, and again. She hit him again, and again. Three times he smacked her, each time more deftly than the one before. Three times she hit him back, each time more viscously than before. Fighting was their love language. She was crying, and the kids sang louder. Suddenly, Lawand grabbed a gun and waved it through the air. Daddy pulled Lawand around by her weave, and she pulled the gun to her chest. He smacked her against the frame of the open window that looked out of the 3-story apartment, shaking the walls. I panicked.

The children's voices grew louder as they danced and played and circled the room. The wind whipped the white curtain out of the way again, just before Daddy pushed Lawand against the window. And she fell. She fell to the floor as I rushed between them and yelled, "Stop it, Daddy!"

"Stop it, Shree?"

"Yeah, stop it, Daddy!"

"I don't know who the hell you think you are tryin' to tell me. Fuck you!"

"Fuck me, Daddy?"

"Yes, fuck you!"

I wanted to be respectful of my father. I loved him. He was a good man at times, and he did so many good things. He showed compassion and love. He called me Princess. But in that moment, in that crowded, sweaty, noisy apartment, I turned and said, "Well, fuck you too."

I am appalled by how those words look on paper, but I want to convey to you the ugliness and brokenness of the situation. All the while, the kids danced and played and sang as if nothing out of the normal happened. I had stepped in to keep Daddy and Lawand from killing each other, only to receive a barrage of F-bombs and to respond in kind. I was broke and homeless now, and my trust was totally broken.

Earlier, when I wrote we all spell struggle the very same way, *s-t-r-u-g-g-l-e*, I didn't mention we all spell *dysfunctional* the same too. You may spell yours with Stoicism, hidden emotions, and alcohol. I spell mine with hand guns and gaiety, F-bombs and pockets full of posy, torn weaves and childhood joy, but all of us, just like the ashes, ashes, we all . . . fall . . . down.

Broken Trust

"Of all the people my heart could have chosen, it decided on a boy who didn't have enough room in his heart to love somebody like me." –a.v.

As I wrote before, I moved to Texas because No Name was familiar and safe. I moved back from Texas because I couldn't find a job, and Texas was neither familiar nor safe. Neither was the home I moved back into, clearly, based on the debacle with my father and Lawand. I moved back in with Momma, back in with the familiar, for a while. But Momma left too, and left me in a dilapidated, old apartment.

I turned nineteen and all the relationships in my life floated about freely; I couldn't ground Momma, couldn't hold Daddy, couldn't reign in No Name, couldn't grasp reality. My existence, from my relationships to my residence, was transient. While attending college, I had a practice of waking up at 3:00 a.m. and crawling out of the bed, knocking roaches to the floor in my drafty apartment that was lit by candlelight, crushing them on the way to the restroom, where I dressed hurriedly before catching the bus to make it to track practice at Los

Angeles Community College by 6:00 a.m. Escape and then stability called to me, then evaded me like a child playing hide-and-seek in the dark.

Mercifully, I met some new friends, Kim and Pam, who seemed genuine. I met them while attending junior college, and they invited me over for dinner. After spending one evening sharing conversation and food, they invited me to stay. I was cloaked in distrust, but I needed a place to stay, and my roach-infested, candlelit apartment was easy to leave. I feared them because I had been betrayed before, and I feared kindness because it had so often been followed by abuse. Maybe they were stable, maybe they wouldn't touch me and leave me. Maybe my life was starting to change a bit, for the better, but my past with my father haunted me. My past with my grandfather haunted me. My past with my stepfather haunted me, but my future with No Name compelled me.

While I lived with Kim and Pam, I conversed with No Name frequently. I learned to trust Kim and Pam and accept them for who they were—genuinely kind people who loved loving people. We celebrated our life together and mourned our losses together. As we grew closer, I felt like No Name drifted slowly away.

No Name remained involved. Although I didn't get to see him play at his university, I did get to see him. Sometimes he would return to L.A. to visit. I think he came to my mother's house just for the fun of it. Momma was always decorating crazy. She might have inflatable palm trees in the kitchen or sea foam orange walls. It was a mess, but no bigger than the mess unraveling in my life.

Shortly before I moved to Tennessee, No Name told me he was a father. I was still his girlfriend at the time, or so I thought, but he now had a daughter. She was three months old. At that time, he represented the most consistent person in my life, but now he too had broken my trust.

Trust is a complex spiderweb stretched across relationships and time. Trust is complex; even while it is firm, it remains tenuously based on your previous relational experiences. Mine had all been broken. One small miscue could cause detachment, rolling the web in upon itself, eventually tearing it down, gravity pulling it to the floor. This time was no different, but it *was* different—I hadn't expected it. With my parents, I had learned to expect it, but not with No Name. Yet No Name told me so nonchalantly, so matter-of-factly, like he didn't expect it to tear my heartstrings. Those words disintegrated the deepest level of trust I had extended to that point in my life, like someone had struck a match just below the web.

No Name and I have a long history together. We hailed from the same fractured universe and battled some of the same monsters and encountered some of the same angels. I wonder if they were ever the same people, those monsters and angels? No Name continued to be a consistent force in my life. He knew every address, he called often, and I did the same. Time transpired and distance grew, but we remained attached, barely. At my graduations, No Name was not there. At my awards ceremonies, No Name was not there, but in my heart, No Name was always there, my heart hanging by a string.

Our lives progressed, mine in Nashville, No Name's in Texas, then a few various states for football: brief stints with the Cincinnati Bengals and Carolina Panthers, some time in Canada, then back to Texas, and finally back to California. He had another child too, but he told me we were still together. Slowly, I discovered I didn't have a place in his world; I had been compartmentalized—I could be his girlfriend on the side, but I could never be his girl. I wasn't enough, or maybe I was too much.

On the tenth anniversary of my brother Daron's murder, I returned to L.A. I had hardly spoken to my father in ten years, but No Name was still there, and we spoke regularly. David and I had met a few weeks earlier, and I had long ago abandoned the hope of being the one girl for No Name, but we remained connected. Something about that childhood friendship, that adolescent love was beautiful and toxic, complicated and wonderful, but mostly conflicted.

No Name picked me up from the airport. We went to Target to pick up some ancillary items, but then he started to grow distant—his sentences shortened, his eyes darted quickly, his posture hardened. I couldn't identify it, but I could feel it. He was pushing me to the periphery again. Was I a threat? Then I felt it. Fear. By now, I knew if he brought me around another girl she would get jealous, or if the timelines of my relationship with him crossed up with the timelines of his relationship with her, he would have some explaining to do—but I still felt used. He avoided taking me to his house. After all these years of constant contact, he wouldn't take me to his house. It was the strangest thing. What was his secret fear?

Later that weekend, he promised to come over to Momma's house for Daron's memorial. Again, it was the strangest thing. He called me and asked what time everything started. He knew what time it started—he had said so the day before. If anything, No Name is not forgetful. He's memorable. He memorizes addresses, phone numbers, everything. He knew what time the memorial started; something else was on his mind. Later, we spoke again, and he said he might not make it until 7:00 or 8:00 p.m. He called again. Now, he said he couldn't make it because it would be disrespectful to show up late.

The boy who had shown up at my house at 2:00 a.m. in the morning just to talk to me was now the man who too afraid to show up at my mother's house after 8:00 p.m. It was indeed the strangest thing. He could have just told me if his girlfriend was upset, but according to No Name, he was never dating anyone, anyway. Even if I asked, "Is there a girl who believes she is in a relationship with you?" the answer was always no.

Why couldn't he just admit that at one time we had a relationship and now it was over? Why was I always a secret? What was the secret this time? I called him on his lies, and we got into a verbal fight. I believe the fight is what he secretly wanted, so he had an excuse not to show up to the house.

I finally talked to him two or three days later, and he confessed: he had had another child. Two years ago. Two years old. No Name and I had talked consistently for the past two years, and he never mentioned his third child. Lies, lies, lies.

I was told when I was a child, "If a man gives you a tennis bracelet, you belong to him, and he loves you." No Name had given me a tennis bracelet. For years, I existed as a hidden person, one with no face and no name in his world. Everyone in my world knew his name. But maybe Daddy was right. Maybe "No Name did have another girl down there." Always. As I said, my relationship with him had been both beautiful and toxic: his eyes told me he loved me, but his lips lied. Today I have moved on, but there is this conflict in me that just wants to be validated, to know I exist in his world, to know I was, at one time, *enough*. Sometimes I ask, "No Name, are you an angel with scars that won't heal, or are you just another monster with a friendly face?" Then I answer myself. *Maybe both.*

Shattered Trust

"Don't worry," she said. "I've spent my whole life falling in love with people who didn't love me back. It's nothing new." –S.Z.

Radio silence. As I mentioned, I had a ten-year period when I didn't talk to my father. I missed him. He was witty and sarcastic and thoughtful at times. I had No Name, but I missed my Daddy. I called him on my thirtieth birthday. My mind was fluttering, ravaged from thinking about some decisions I had made during a difficult time when I was nineteen. By the time I was thirty, the pain of that decision had taken a toll on me, so I decided to call him and tell him how grateful I was he and Momma didn't have an abortion with me.

"Dad."

"Yeah, Princess."

"You know, um, I know it must have been hard when you found out Momma was pregnant. I umm, I know you might not have wanted to have me. I know it was Momma's first time and all, so it couldn't have been easy for either of you."

"Uh-huh."

"Dad, I know no woman thinks she is gonna' get pregnant the first time she has sex, but Momma did. I know you were surprised."

"Uh-huh."

"Dad?"

"Yeah, Princess."

"Dad, thanks for not having an abortion when you found out. Thanks for keeping me alive and letting Momma have the baby. I just wanted to say thanks—"

"Princess! Why do you keep sayin' all that about it bein' Frankie's first time and all? She's a freak! That weren't the first time she had sex!"

No Name

About six months before I began writing this book, I spoke with No Name, and he told me he had another child who was now two years old. Before I got married, he would tell me I was better than all these guys I was dating. He would validate me over the phone or to my face, but never in front of other people. If I was so dope, why didn't he ever just swoop in and rescue me? Was it the jealousy of the other women? Did he ever really value me? My hidden stature in his life tells me no. Probably not. Maybe.

Daddy

Lawand died on April 1, 2016. Ironically, Momma worried she might need Lawand's help in case she died when the kids were young, but Lawand went first. I flew to California to visit Daddy and be supportive. One of the dynamics of our dysfunctional relationship expressed itself through my father being overly considerate of his stepchildren, but not me.

Before the funeral, I was at my father's house when Lawand's daughter approached me, "Shree, you not in the 'bituary because I didunt' want chu in there. If you was wonderin' about that, that's me. That's why y'all three ain't in the 'bituary, that's me!"

I told her I respected her opinion and I understood. I kept looking at my father to see if he would tell her to back off or jump to my defense. He didn't. He just sat there.

The onslaught continued. For two hours she came at me with taunts and provoking comments. Daddy never said anything. The afternoon wore on. While I was in the garage with my father and grandmother, I heard a shrill "Shree!" so loud we all looked at each other simultaneously. Lawand's daughter stood in the doorway, with her middle finger extended, accentuated by a long, crusty nail overdue for a manicure, circling her body. She pursed her lips around her front teeth and bulged her eyes. Her body language said, "Come and get some!" Daddy just looked away.

No Name

Conflicted, conflicted, conflicted. That's how I felt. I wanted to exist in No Name's world. I just wanted to know I have a name in his world. I was supposed to be his girlfriend, but he never broke up—with me. Maybe I was stuck mentally at age seventeen. I wondered if this was some type of sick, sexual soul-tie with dysfunction, or if I were stuck in my childlike fantasy. I thought I mattered.

When I first started dating No Name, he was living with his mom again. She was comfortable. She struggled with many different issues, but she made time for me. She was fond of me. She would tell me not to wear my heart on my sleeve, attached with strings. Maybe it was a warning—don't trust, they'll break your heart and leave you stranded every time.

Daddy

My father once left me stranded. In 2014, I went to visit him for his birthday. I didn't tell anyone I was going or coming, not even Momma. Especially not Momma. When I arrived, I went out to my father's house to surprise him. We spent the weekend together. I wanted to take him out to dinner, but he wouldn't let me, wouldn't you know it? He was afraid of what Lawand's kids might think.

I told him when I was out there David had proposed. He was so excited; he grabbed me, kissed my face and said, "Princess, I want to walk you down the aisle."

Now, I have tried not to have expectations for my father. Since he didn't show at my sixth-grade graduation or at any of my special events, I didn't have expectations. And I quit placing any on him. But this time, he volunteered, his terms.

As the day approached, he started making excuses. He didn't know about flying all that way. He didn't want to upset Lawand's kids. I told him, "Dad, you volunteered for this. If you want out, you're going to have to tell me to my face." I would ask him if he had his tickets, and he would tell me no. He started asking about our colors, and then he would question, "Why did you pick those colors?"

I thought this time would be different, but he started acting strange. I could tell he didn't want to come. Maybe fear?

No Name

The message behind my relationship with No Name was I was good enough for the side and good enough for the ride, but not good enough for his life. The pain wasn't in the rejection; the pain was in the message the rejection sent. I was not good *enough*.

But I still care for No Name even today. I consider what might have happened, what might have hurt him so badly. I contemplate what happened to that young boy who was so extremely driven, so incredibly talented, and so dearly present that he would sit by my side in the candlelight while I struggled through my homework. Where was that man who protected me and was present with me when we were kids? I have forgiven him.

Daddy

About two weeks before my wedding I got a text. It was from my father, and it read, "Hey, Princess. I am in my feelings right now. Please don't call me, but I wanted to let you know I am not coming to your wedding." I read the message while sitting in my chair at work, and I kept it together, but I blew snot and tears and cried and screamed when I got home to David. I was ashamed. I was angry. I wasn't angry with Daddy; I was angry with myself for having believed him.

Daddy and No Name

They are the same person, No Name and my father. I saw my father keep me a secret in his life, and I saw No Name do the same. I felt them show me through their actions I was not enough. I watched as my father could conjure up the emotion and gumption to provide for and be considerate of his stepchildren, but not for me. No Name did the same for those other women. Dad and No Name are the same person. On the other hand, maybe they aren't the same person; maybe I am the same person and they treat me the same. I am not saying it is my fault, what I am saying is my love was unconditional, and to them, that was a sign to take advantage.

I call my father "Daddy," and he calls me "Princess," but I have often been the orphan. I call No Name by his real name, and he calls me "Ree," but I have no name in his world, and he asked to remain nameless in mine. The boy with the pretty face and no name, the dad with no words but great game, and the girl with no name and no name.

Lewis B. Smedes wrote, "To forgive is to set a prisoner free and discover the prisoner was you." That's what I had to do. I had to forgive Dad and No Name, and I've done it. I still wonder, though, I wonder what happened to them, I wonder what hurt them so deeply inside that they can't fully give of themselves, and why they mask, and lie, and cover up. I hurt for them too. Something must have hurt them, shaken them, stained them to the core, to keep them from standing up for me. I know they must be broken and scarred, and I love them both.

But eventually I did learn that real men can stand up.

Torn Trust

"Windows break, mirrors shatter, but hearts . . . they tear, and never cleanly." –M.I.

On April 10, 2014, while driving to pick up my 1966 Ford Mustang, my phone rang. I had fallen in love with that car when I turned sixteen, purchased one in 2007, ran into several restoration issues, and sold it in 2014. In the aftermath of my father's wedding day give-away cancelation, I took joy in purchasing my new, old love—that car.

I answered the phone just before I arrived at the dealer; the voice on the other end was Momma's. I asked, "Can I call you back once I pick up the car?"

"Cool, but call me back. I need to talk to you!"

My mind flooded with thoughts, my hands grew clammy, the steering wheel started to stick to my hands. *What could be going on now*?

Once I got home, I called her before I even opened the door to the car.

"Shree, you got a pen?"

"No, Momma, I don't have a pen, but I can get one."

"When you get a pen, I need you to write down these numbers. Do you have a pen? I need you to write down these numbers."

"Okay, Momma, I got a pen."

"Write down these numbers. I sent you some money."

"What?"

"Write down these numbers, I sent you some money with MoneyGram. I sent you $550."

"What?"

"I sent you $550."

Long pause . . .

"You're not comin' to the weddin'?"

"Well, I sent you $550."

"You're not coming to the wedding? Okay, Momma."

Click.

I fell to the floor and cried. Not because I was angry; no, not because I was angry, but because I had believed them. I was shame. Everyone told me this would be different. Everyone told me a wedding was different. But they didn't show up. They never showed up . . .

Standing Trust

"Don't be scared to change the prince's name in your story." –Atticus

The moment I walked down the aisle on my wedding day, I looked at the last man standing. Actually, several men were standing—the whole room was standing, but four men were standing up for me.

The first was, of course, David. While others had come and gone like the tide, sloshed in and out like dirty water from a wash bucket, and evaporated like steam off a mirror, David stood. In one of the moments when I felt the most abandoned by my parents, David stood up.

The second was Reginald, David's father. Consistently, he had tried to step in and father me, love me, show me what it is like to be loved unconditionally by a man with no ulterior motive. And on our wedding day, he stood up for his son. He stood for me too.

The last two were Robert and Michael. Robert was my next-door neighbor, whose house I went to on the night I thought David broke up—*Worst. Proposal. Ever.* Michael, again, is Robert's partner. Michael and Robert walked me down the aisle and gave me away. They weren't just standing, they were walking it out with me.

Robert and Michael were busy professionals with busy lives just like David and I were. They were busy, but they still wanted to help with the wedding, so David and I gladly let them. After Dad bailed, I prepared to walk down the aisle by myself; I didn't need anyone to do it after he canceled. I would be covered by the Father, Son, and Holy Spirit, and my heart grew in gratitude. God was enough and still I felt I should share my gratitude with people for the parts they played in my life. So one morning when we took time on a Saturday out of our schedules to have a quick brunch, I began to cry right there in front of David, Robert, and Michael. All three of them looked at me with concern, and I asked them: "Robert, Michael, would you two be willing to walk me down the aisle?" They said yes, and we all cried together, but me most of all.

Not only did they walk me down the aisle, they helped plan the engagement party. When I tell you they set it out, they set it out! The paid for a violinist, had the whole thing catered, ordered some of the best champagne and wine, even served prime rib. On the way to the church on my wedding day, they asked what music I wanted to listen to, and I told them, "The Curse Is Broken" by James Fortune. Again, we cried. The past did not define me. My shattered relationships did not define me. The past was not who I was. I was Shree, and I was among friends. Some people question it. "Why did you have two gay men walk you down the aisle?" Some give disconcerting looks when I mention a gay couple walked me down the aisle. I imagine people have judged me. *What is this? Your way of showing off your progressive thinking by having two gay men walk you down the aisle? I thought you were . . . Christian?*

I avoid verbal sparring; it's no good. My story is not a place for me to declare my stance on homosexuality, nor do I believe I need to. What is written is written—all manner of behaviors and thoughts have been condemned—I encourage people to look it up for themselves. Michael and Robert honored me that day; they were then and they still are my friends. In the absence of my father and my mother, they honored me—they walked me down the aisle and gave me away! Talk about standing up for orphans.

I read somewhere once, that love, it covers a multitude of sins. I am not sure I really know what that means. Do the sins get atoned for? Are they overshadowed? Is God more forgiving of one who sins often but loves much? I don't really know. However, when I think back on that day, and I think about men, real men, standing up, I wonder: who was more Christ-like in that moment? My father? Or Robert and Michael?

Shattered

"Let him in whose ears the low-voiced Best is killed by the clash of the First,
Who holds that if way to the Better there be, it exacts a full look at the Worst,
Who feels that delight is a delicate growth cramped by crookedness, custom and fear,
Get him up and be gone as one shaped awry; he disturbs the order here."
–Thomas Hardy "*In Tenebris* II"

My relationship with my father has been tepid at its best times and calculatingly cold at its worst. Momma pushed me out and reeled me back in. No Name did the same. Women used me, molested me. Men abused me, raped me, denigrated me. My closest family and friends often caused the greatest harm. I will look at the shattered relationships, but I will not be defined by them.

I've told you stories of my mother and father, the monster with the friendly face, No Name, and others, but I have also interwoven stories of my grandmother, David and his parents, Robert and Michael, Jessica, my students, and friends. Each relationship is unique, redemptive in many ways—like with Grandma and Momma—but in some of them I see repetition—the relationship shatters in the end. With none of them do I regret the friendship, the laughter, the good times, nor the love I gave, even if it cost me dearly. I will choose to look at the shattered relationships, but I will also choose find the dear rest and not the tears.

Walking Away

Walking is one of the exercises we avoid: parking as close to the store as possible, taking the elevator, ordering delivery, but walking can be a wonderful experience. Walking gives us time to think when our body is also in motion. It is a task that requires very little brain-power, but it pays vast dividends—it takes us where we need to go, away from what we want to avoid, into a calorie-burning state, into a realm where we can think, and wonder, and hope. I have spent thousands of hours walking, but just recently have I learned to walk away.

Earlier, I told of two men who loved me unconditionally, stood up for me, loved me, and walked me down the aisle—Robert and Michael. Sadly, our relationship at this point is not as whole as it once was. One more relationship shattered, one more lesson to learn.

I never judged Robert for his relationships. I have always been friends with an eccentric group of people—Robert was no different—I just loved him more. The day I purchased my first home in 2012, I ran around in it just praising: "Jesus, Jesus, Jesus!" My feet floated across the floor and my heart bellowed into the ceiling. The sound cascaded down the stairs and filled the room beneath me. Yes, I wrote, *down the stairs*, because this girl, this misfit from L.A. who barely made it through school, who lived this nomadic lifestyle, who was perpetually abandoned, purchased a two-story home in Nashville. Coming from my family, buying a new home was monumental!

I ascended out onto the roof and gazed at the wide and wonderful city around me, the light glinting off the other rooftops, streetlights, and window panes. The wind blew lightly across my face as I began to twirl around in the wonder of the spring sun warming my face, beckoning my praise. Silence came, but it was not a stark silence; this silence was calm, peaceful, and light. My heart stopped for joy, and I turned to see a man peering at me from under his hat through his bedroom window.

"Excuse me!" I called. "Excuse me, sir?" He opened the window. "Do you have a wine bottle opener?" And Robert and I became fast friends.

We did everything together: birthday parties, Memorial Day, Independence Day, Halloween, Thanksgiving, Christmas, New Year's, and anything else we could find to celebrate at the time. We would sneak over to each other's homes to play karaoke, dress-up, or any old thing because we were friends. Along came David, and he fit right in. Along came Michael, and he fit right in. We grew up as adults together.

Even though we had all the parties and good times together, we did have a few awkward moments. One time when we were all at Robert and Michael's, Robert was at the stove working on some lasagna he had pulled out of the oven; he made a quick gesture, turned, and fed some of the lasagna to Michael. Quick as a flash, he dug out another piece and turned toward David. Robert was going to hand the fork to David, but David was confused and just stood there. He opened his mouth. The lasagna fell to the floor and Michael and I busted up laughing. Robert looked at David, raised one eyebrow and said, "You cute, but you are not my type at all!"

Family is not a word defined simply by blood. *Family* is defined by a love for each other that protects, comforts, prods, teaches, and doesn't let go. Robert and Michael became my family. I finally felt like I belonged, like I fit. The misfit was gone and the retrofit was here to stay. We walked out life together, and then somebody tripped.

David and I always started with Robert and Michael. If we planned a party or to go out, the list always started and ended with Robert and Michael, as did the usual evenings. Our inside jokes, intimate messages of laughter to one another with just a word, look, or wink, were always shared with Robert and Michael. We were like a four-leaf clover, unexpected, exceedingly rare, yet perfectly bland if one of the clovers was missing. Although we were busy, we made time for each other in spite of our careers and educational pursuits. We kept spending time together, even after it got really weird.

On Father's Day, I took Robert, Michael, and David out. We shared a few drinks, a meal, tons of laughter, and good conversation. Somehow Robert mentioned a few special friends had planned an engagement party for Robert and Michael. I hadn't even heard of it, and . . . We. Weren't. Invited. We weren't invited. The situation felt odd, eerie even, as if an uninvited guest had shown up and interrupted the conversation. He had. His name was Jealousy.

I asked them about the party and they made it sound like everything was cool, but a wall had ascended, quickly. A few weeks later, I heard about some mutual friends throwing Robert a massive bachelor party. Apparently, again, we weren't invited. I made contact with the friend who had planned the party, and she forwarded me the invitation. The invitations had been sent out in June. It was August. I asked her why I wasn't invited, and she said I would have to talk to Robert. The party eclipsed huge, spanning three to four days. I was flabbergasted.

The next morning, the phone rang. Robert was calling . . .

"Hello?"

"Shree, you up?"

"Hi, Robert! Yes, I am up. How are you?"

"I hear you were upset because you didn't get invited to the party."

"Well . . . yes, Robert, I am a little upset I didn't get invited to the party. We always celebrate together; we do everything together. Did I do something wrong? Did I hurt you in some way?"

"No, Shree, you didn't do anything wrong. This party, well, umm, there are lots of people coming in for this party. Lots of people coming in from out of town. You know, people we haven't seen in a while . . ."

"Go on."

"Well, we, um, Shree, uh . . . we couldn't invite everyone. They just, kind of put it together last minute here and I, um, didn't get to invite everyone. It was just too much at once. A lot of people are coming in from out of town. Uh . . . we'll have another party, Shree."

"Okay, Robert, you don't have to defend yourself to me."

Silence.

"Robert?"

"Yeah."

"Love you, Robert."

"Love you too. Goodbye, Shree."

"Bye, Robert."

And that was it. The conversation, the party, the e-mail invitation. Nothing added up. David was livid. He was ready to sever ties. I wasn't.

On the eve of the bachelor's party, I got a text that read, "Come on over." *Weird. Now he is texting me?* I told David and we argued. We went anyway. We socialized for about thirty-five minutes and felt incredibly awkward. There were no pictures that night for us, no dancing, no toasts, no laughing, only shattered expectations. We said our goodbyes, walked down the stairs, out the door, and back home, alone.

The wedding felt the same—awkward. We were not invited, in other words, we were uninvited—previously guaranteed to be on the list, but now intentionally placed on the other list—placed on the do-not-call list. Beautifully arranged with flowers and glass and candles everywhere, the wedding exceeded expectations for décor and pizzazz. The night before the wedding, David and I sat at home. A mutual friend kept texting me to come over, but I responded, "Where are you?" Twenty minutes later, Robert texted, "Y'all coming over for drinks?" David and I stayed put this time. David had steam rising up from under his collar into the crisp autumn air. I looked cool as a frosted glass externally, but inside, I churned a whirlpool of emotions.

The cool September breeze turned to the blustery October winds, followed by the cold November rains in Nashville. The dark, ominous clouds that drape over the city during the winter months descended, and Halloween and Thanksgiving wandered by without so much as a phone call. Everyone was busy. In November, David's mom passed away. Robert and Michael came to the home, but then faded into nothingness. No phone calls, no texts, no smiles, nor laughs were exchanged. They just walked away.

So I reached out to them and pulled Robert in. Robert had opened the door a crack by sending me a text, and I responded with, "For the life of me I cannot figure out why we stopped talking. You are missed!" At that time, that was the best I could do to reach out. Robert understood and responded. He invited me to a wonderful place called Hemmingway's, where we shared a drink. I asked him what happened, and again, I felt Jealousy sneak back into the room, peering over my shoulder, or maybe his.

"Shree, you know, you know. Things changed. We, we were getting frustrated. Stuff happened. You, you and David. Well, we felt like y'all were taking advantage of us, you know, using us."

As those words split his lips and fell on my ears, my temperature rose and my heart bottomed out. The back of my neck began to sweat and the tops of my ears tingled. In one, quick, deliberate swoop, I unloaded the past six months on him. I reminded him of all the times we brought food, drinks, gifts, everything to his house. I reminded him how David and I would stop by, even if just for five or ten minutes, to say hello. I told him how I would stop working on my dissertation just to spend time with them. I would put my work and my social calendar on hold for them. I reminded them of when we went canoeing, and David forgot his cash; that same day we went to the ATM and paid them back more than we borrowed. David used to question me about why I brought over so much to their house, why I always seemed to be trying to do more for them, and I told him, "Michael always talks about this one friend who takes advantage of them. I don't want to be that one friend."

He listened patiently, but I grew sweaty, my hands hot and clammy because I know I am a lot of things. I am self-centered and selfless, I am impulsive and kind, I am reticent and effusive, but I am not inconsiderate of my friends. Period.

For a while, I felt like Robert and I shared a heart, but that feeling has since been shattered. I miss him dearly, and Michael too, and I am not sure what either of us did wrong. I don't believe they did anything wrong other than getting offended. I don't believe we did anything wrong other than getting offended.

I did learn two important principles from this relationship. First, let me say that I do not believe the relationships are permanently severed, and it is my eternal hope that we will reconnect as friends, stronger than before. I want my brothers back. Now, what I learned was this: people who talk about people will talk about people. If someone talks negatively about others, he or she will talk negatively about others, including friends and family. Nobody is absolved. The second thing I learned is that sometimes I have to walk away. Walking is good; walking helps us pick up the broken pieces. Walking helps us reset and rest in the shattered dreams of today. Walk on, and maybe, just maybe we can walk back the way we came, back into each other's arms, tomorrow.

I believe in reconciliation; I believe in the possibilities. Walking away is not an end, it's a beginning. I look back over my relationship with Robert and Michael and I choose to remember the good. The pictures, the laughter, the gifts are all reminders of what once was, and what, if we believe in the possibilities, can be again.

Steady

"Out of the broken came something whole. Out of the hurting came something healing."–Unknown

When I finished writing the chapter on my shattered relationships with Robert and Michael, I came to a critical juncture. The chronicle of my healing lay placidly in the first few chapters while my narrative of my broken relationships careened through the final few chapters. A give and take emerged, a balancing act, healing and helplessness wound up tightly in one package. But something evaded me, something was missing. I added to the memoir, searching for a piece I misplaced, and brought myself full circle to the present and the deterioration of my relationship with my two good friends, Robert and Michael. Yet something remained. One giant relationship loop loomed about in my head. I saw the need to demonstrate relationships are not completely good or bad, broken or whole. Instead, relationships are like a long walk—ups, downs, falls, euphoria, and often monotony. In my life, relationships have had three stages: shattered, steady, and recovery.

The autumn leaves turned from green, gold, yellow, and orange to brown, solid brown. When I started Fisk University in the fall of 1998 everyone seemed to be brown, and my being a deep, dark brown created a sense of separation. My skin was darker than the paper bag once used to grant admission at historically black colleges. So was hers. In the past, light skin helped earn a student admission, and when I first came to Fisk light skin still elicited respect, esteem, and at times a place in a sorority or fraternity. Her skin soaked in the atmosphere unapologetically, like she did, a personality full of statements, without question, and a determined force. My new friend Lia's personality pulsed loudly and pushed itself on me, but she didn't overwhelm me—I just always knew she was there.

We were suitemates, but on this day in late October, we decided to become roommates. We spent so much time in each other's rooms, we naturally began to migrate into one. All of the girls in our suite discussed it, and for the interest of all parties involved, we decided to swap roommates. And it was a party.

Lia's personality can be in your face, but not like an angry black woman; rather, she is a no-nonsense, kind-hearted, and listening friend to whom I am forever indebted. Our time on campus and in the dorm room increased, and our friendship blossomed, as if fed by the fertilizer of time. After my experience with Kim and Pam, two wonderful friends who served me and did not take advantage of me, I grew more willing to share myself again with other people. Lia and I developed the type of relationship where you tell each other everything. One night, I did. I told her about being abused as a child.

"When I tell you my body and my mind disconnected in that moment, it was surreal. It was like I had an out-of-body experience. I was ten feet off the floor watching myself perform this act on this man, and suspended in the air. I cried for myself. But on earth I never cried loud enough for anyone to hear me."

"You didn't scream?"

"No, Lia, I didn't scream. I was stuck. I was barely seven years old. I couldn't scream. I was a child. I was afraid. I couldn't scream or bite or pinch. I could only perform."

"You couldn't just bite him, take a piece of him with you? You couldn't holler for your Momma? I don't know, Ree, I would have done something."

"You don't know that, Lia. You don't know that until you've been in the situation. You don't know that . . ."

"Ree, I am sorry, but I know me. I would have done *something*."

Lia listened, and she understood; only she couldn't comprehend why I hadn't fought back. In her world, in her experience, she always swung first. Our relationship continued to deepen and Lia became my best friend. Beside No Name, she spent more time with me and knew me more intimately than anyone else. We lived together. Later, we even moved off campus into a rental home with one other friend, who was a few years younger.

We all worked and we all attended Fisk and had busy, busy lives. Something unique about our new roommate was that she had an involved father—one who paid attention, some tuition, and visits often. He ordered food for us, gave gifts sometimes, maintained entertaining conversation, took us out to dinner, and made it apparent his daughter was a priority. To Lia and me, this new territory was enviable. Our dads never came to visit, or called, or cared for that matter.

One evening, we had some company over and decided to take the night off from doing schoolwork. Part-time and full-time jobs, school, and the pressures of survival had worn us thin. Our new roommate worked late, overnight, but her dad decided to spend the night, even without her there.

For all intents and purposes, the night expired normally, and the sun arose again on a new day. I crept out of the bedroom and past the kitchen to see one of our guests off for the morning. When my feet shuffled on the linoleum floor, I heard a faint whisper, a beg for my attention, "Ree! Ree!" I looked to Lia's door, but it remained staunchly closed. I swore I had heard her.

"Ree! Ree!"

I looked to my right, and she stood there, hunched forward in her nightgown, holding her sugarberry, tears in her eyes.

"Ree! Ree! I am so sorry. I am so sorry."

"Lia, what are you talking about? Why are you up so early, and why are you out here crying? Why are you sorry?"

"Ree, I couldn't say anything. I couldn't move. I couldn't do anything. I just froze up. I lay there. I was so scared. I was so scared."

"Take it easy, Lia. What are you talking about? Who hurt you?"

"Shhh! He's still in there."

"Who?"

"Our roommate's dad."

"What the hell? In where? In your room? He's in your room? What's he doin' in your room? Lia, what the hell?"

"He came in there last night. He came in there. He came in there."

"It's okay, it's okay, what do you want me to do?"

"He came in there. He came in there and he got in the bed with me. I pretended to be asleep, but he wouldn't leave me alone. He kept touching me, putting his sick hands all over me. He tried to pry my legs open, but I squeezed them and rolled over."

"Did he? Did he get in?"

"No, he never got in. I kept pretending to be asleep, but he never left. I couldn't yell. I was so afraid. Oh, Ree, I am so sorry. I am so sorry."

"Lia, why are you sorry? You didn't do anything wrong. It's his fault, not yours."

"No. I am sorry because I couldn't yell. I told you that you should have, but I couldn't do it. You were a little kid; I am a grown woman, and I couldn't yell. Couldn't do anything. I was so scared."

Trauma bond. A true phenomenon. Lia and I loved each other before this incident, but after the incident, our friendship fused. We fused together over academics, journey, and triumph, but we also fused together over trauma, our loss of voice, our feelings of total isolation and powerlessness when another person tried to own us.

We cried together, and we helped each other, and our friendship fused. I finally had someone I could help, someone I understood, someone I could try to help ease the pain.

We three roommates remained friends, but Lia and I grew much closer than before. Our other roommate apologized to Lia for her father's actions, but as is typical with sexual abuse, nothing ever happened to the perpetrator. We never saw him again. Eventually, we all moved on with our lives, but Lia and I remained close.

Bonded

Bonds can be formed by heat, such as when welding together two metals, or bonds can be formed by cold, such as a tongue and a flagpole. Bonds can be formed by friction (which creates heat), such as between a man and a woman or between magnesium and aluminum alloys. Time, proximity, and a mutual journey can form bonds too, so Lia and I formed a stronger, more resilient relationship through time, intentional proximity, and walking out this life together.

Lia finished Fisk and went to work for DSHS. I began teaching, joined the Navy, went back to school, but we still progressed through life together. Over the years, Lia had two children I loved dearly, especially the older son, Amari.

On July 14, 2013, the day before what would have been my brother Daron's birthday, my phone rang. It was Lia.

"I need a ride! Amari! Accident! Alabama! I need! A ride! Alabama! Accident!"

The mumbled, muffled, sounds coming from my phone screamed hysteria in my ear. I held the phone far away, trying to discern the message.

"Calm down, Lia, calm down. I can't understand you? What do—"

"Amari! Ride! Alabama!"

"I heard you, do you need—"

"Amari! Amari! Amari!"

My feet wore the rug thin, pacing back and forth, back and forth. For ten minutes I tried to get her to calm down. I agreed to give her a ride to Alabama—I would have anyway, but I couldn't understand her. I called David immediately. We were not married at the time, just dating, but I needed help. In the morning, I had a very important meeting with a group of principals and I have to give the presentation. I called David close to 9:00 p.m. We had to drive to Alabama that night in the dark, on no sleep, and try to make it back to my house before the presentation. And I still didn't know what was wrong.

We picked up Lia and her younger son from her house, and although she acted much calmer, her demeanor and temperament showed a frazzled mess.

"Amari's been in an accident. His dad drove, his cousin rode shotgun, and Amari sat in the back seat. Now he is in surgery. He's going to make it, but he had some head trauma. My phone's dead now. I forgot my charger."

"Okay," I said, "we'll get you down there, but I have to come back tomorrow for my meeting."

"I know. I know. Thank you for taking me. He was so excited. He was so excited to go to Alabama with his dad, and now this. I hope he's okay."

The drive grew long, tired, and ominous. The conversation lessened and disappeared. Everyone's emotions wore thin, drained by worry and helplessness. Lia remained quiet. She didn't sleep, but she didn't speak either.

Three hours later we arrived at the hospital, anxiety now residing as a lump in our throat and a gurgle in our stomachs. David waited outside while Lia, her son, and I stole quickly through the hospital breezeway and into the front entrance under the dark sky and white lights.

The entrance desk was a nightmare. Uniformed, slow, stalling clerks took fifteen minutes to locate Amari's room. We almost left, believing we had arrived at the wrong hospital, when a middle-aged lady, dressed in black came and grabbed Lia by the hand and said, "Let's go upstairs." She knew where Amari's room was. More waiting. We went to the room, but Amari had disappeared. No. This room was another waiting room. Amari was not here either.

Waiting. The lady in black asked to take Lia's younger son into another room. Waiting. The doctor emerged. Tensions clung to the ceiling and scraped their fingernails against the walls. The anxiety in the throat had grown into an acid ball, burning its way out to our pores, moistening our eyes.

We sat. The doctor explained.

"Amari rode in the back seat. He was lying prone on the bench seat, unbuckled, when the tire blew and the sudden loss of velocity propelled him from the car with great force. The landing caused massive head trauma. We took him into surgery. I'm sorry. We couldn't save him."

The gurgle in our stomachs and the fire in our throats erupted with Lia's wails. She cried for her baby and her pain emanated into the waiting room walls. The lady in black turned into the chaplain, the stalling made sense, and the waiting had only delayed the inevitable breakdown. Lia screamed and cried, "Let me see him! Let me see him!" I looked at the doctor and shook my head no. I made sure he saw me. "Let me see him! Let me see him!" She consumed the room. I climbed up on the couch and jumped on her back to keep her from hurting herself. I clamped down. I wouldn't let go. I held on.

When I tell you, when I tell you she was in pain, in so much pain; when I tell you she was in so much pain . . .

We fell to the floor, my legs wrapped around her torso, and we cried. And we held. And part of her died.

We went in the room to see Amari. His head was . . . his head was so badly . . . his head . . .

When I tell you she was in so much pain . . .

David sent a text. I sent one back. Amari was gone. David broke down. His son was ten years old also. He wanted to stay, but we had to go.

I left my friend that night and we drove back to Nashville. I didn't sleep. I gave my presentation, disappeared out the back door, drove to Lia's house, cleaned up for her return and waited.

Part of her returned.

Lia is my most steady friend. We have maintained our friendship for more than twenty years now. We still talk and see each other regularly. I guess you could say we are knit together at the soul. I don't fear her leaving and she doesn't fear my leaving. We're bonded. Albeit by trauma, and friction, and heat, and cold, and pain, and death, we're also bonded by joy, love, friendship, hope, and empathy. We've held hands through all of this, and the autumn leaves turn brown again every year.

Recovery

"I have late night conversations with the moon, he tells me about the sun and I tell him about you."–S. L. Gray

The moon is a weird object in the sky, orbiting the earth, which orbits the sun, yet the moon lights the earth at night as it reflects the light from the sun. The moon is so tangible, so close, something we reach for, to touch, to hold, to walk upon. The sun is a gaseous ball of flames, burning, ever burning, providing light and growth to the earth, but also scorching and singeing away life, water, and breath. We appreciate the sunrise and the sunset, but we curse the overhead sun. We worship it with our bodies but hide from it our hearts. Our hearts are reserved for the moon.

My mother gets a bad rap. My writing has given her this. She gave birth to three children by the time she was nineteen and three more before she was thirty. We moved countless times, and in my nineteenth year, she left me for another man. She didn't come to my wedding, but now she's here. Now I see how she emerged at the sunrise of her life and returned at the sunset of her life—and in the middle she burnt brightly, trying to survive.

Frankie is not Momma's given name. As the story goes, she commandeered the name Frankie because she walked like Frankenstein—I have my doubts. Momma turned fifteen when I was born; she was still a baby, a kid in high school. As I wrote before, she mothered three children by the age of nineteen; however, what I didn't include was Momma managed to finish high school in spite of having three kids. Momma exuded resiliency.

Momma braided hair and had conversations constantly. As she braided everyone's hair, she listened well, thought logically, and explained issues with empathy and candor. More than once I heard her giving counsel on how to make blended families work, how to show forgiveness, and how to keep the peace. Women loved Momma because her charisma overtook them, and she listened too. Momma, the life of the party, the fly on the wall, made her own big, hairy mess, while helping everyone else straighten her own.

I can remember riding in the car with her, going to Huntington Park to shop, and I stared at her, admiring her, thinking about how beautiful she looked. I couldn't see myself in Momma that day, but I learned to; however, on that day I only admired her and not my reflection of her. We had gone to Huntington Park before my sixth-grade graduation to go dress shopping. In my house, sixth-grade graduation represented a rite of passage into junior high. Daddy couldn't make it, but Momma went all out.

We arrived at Huntington Park and I designed a dress. Oh, that dress. I loved that dress. The dress clashed with my culture because it looked like a quinceañera dress, mint green, with lace going down the middle, like doilies, and a tiara on my head. The purchase of the dress created a rift between my siblings and me—it seemed as if I had received special treatment, but what the gift said to me was Momma would do whatever it took to make my graduation special.

Momma loved people and she loved sports. We constantly had company over because our house was the house where music played, dominoes were played, kids played, and sports were played. A savant at dominoes, Momma was really a competition freak. I used to leave the room during the Laker games because she would pass out on the bed, turn the television off and on, coach both the coaches and the players, scream at the refs, and then fake-faint all over again. Momma loved sports drama.

I used to roll my eyes and sigh when I thought about it, until I started thinking about tetherball, track, drill team, ROTC, and any other competition I got my hands on. Momma's competitive streak became my competitive streak. She loved to dance, and she taught me the Cha-Cha. I love to dance now. Momma dug Luther Vandross, so do I. She cared about her appearance, she wanted to be dressed and pressed, so do I. Momma took care of her own and usually took care of other people's babies too. I am a teacher. Today I see myself in Momma.

Momma also cried. When I told her about the abuse, she and Grandma flew over to Auntie Bailey's and held me and cried. Well, Momma cried. Grandma got angry. Momma made it clear she didn't know, she didn't know he had touched me, she would have stopped it. Momma cried for me, but she cried for herself too. She wanted to be a good mother.

I realize Momma fought hard for everything we had. She survived. Six children, in L.A., braiding hair, no husband, Momma fought hard the best she knew how. She fought for our lives and hers too. Sometimes all the fighting made her get in her own way.

For seven years, I never saw Momma, but things changed. She apologized for her relationships, especially the one with Michael—the man for whom she left Otis—and I matured. I tried to walk a mile in her shoes and she tried to walk a mile in mine. After my wedding, Momma and I started to talk more often. We began to communicate openly. She came to my graduation party a few years ago, and although jealousy consumed her as I previously described, the important part is she came. And she stayed. And she adjusted to the pressure of the other women.

A few months ago, Momma moved to Nashville. We talk often and see each other weekly. We go to movies together, and we are repairing our relationship. Sometimes when I look at her, I see me. In her eyes, in her smile, in her witty responses, I see a reflection of myself. But as I have recently discovered, again, life is not all about me. Momma came first. When I look at her, I don't see a reflection of myself—it is the other way around. When I look at her, I see her, and I see the sun. I am the moon, and I reflect the good that Momma shines on me. Ours is a relationship in repair, and we believe in the possibilities.

The moon orbits the earth, and the earth orbits the sun, which lights up the earth by day and the moon by night. I hope, one day, Momma and I can stand hand in hand looking at the Son who lights up the world—together.

Trauma

Move

"A home cannot exist without a heart, and a heart is at full ease once it finally finds its home." –M.I.

To analyze is to break down an item into its constituent parts for closer examination or study. A house is easy to analyze: door, frame, floor, ceiling, walls, lights, television, closet, bathroom, kitchen, window. A home is less easy to analyze: belonging, peace, richness, aroma, pain, sickness, disease, abuse, confidence, demise, joy, restlessness, violence, apparition, fading, gone. I have lived in many houses, apartments, and condos, but until now, I have had only one home, and that was 2248 E. 92nd Street, in the Jordan Downs Housing Community.

Jordan Downs is a set of government subsidized housing lovingly called the projects. The particular location of this project was south of Central Avenue, a.k.a. South Central. Made famous by movies such as *Menace II Society, Colors, Friday, Boyz n the Hood,* and *South Central,* the area gained an iconic reputation as the quintessential gangsta's paradise. Furthermore, gangsta rap music created such a stigma most people thought South Central was a city or suburb of L.A.

Really, South Central comprised an area, an idea, an energy, and my first and only childhood home.

The projects were enigmatic. From the exterior they threatened violence, drugs, and death. Gangs infested ours. On a Crip gang street, I often heard, "Who ride gansta, Crip?" or read the graffiti tag on some lonely building. We also had some Latino gangs: the Watts Varrio Grape 13 and F13. Police helicopters flew by at low altitudes, drug busts happened regularly, and there were two primary colors—black and brown.

But that was from the outside. Inside the projects, although gangs resided there, violence happened, and drugs were sold and used, a whole different story played out. Don't be confused; the two main colors were black and brown, not black and blue. So let me take you on a ride, as Coolio so coldly borrowed from Lakeside, on a "fantastic voyage" to my crib on the South Side.[1]

In the Ghetto

Historically, there have been all types of ghettos—places where specified groups of people lived. Jewish people were forced to live outside Italy in ghettos. In the Appalachian Mountains, ghettos of Caucasian people gathered and lived in "hollers" for centuries. In South Central Los Angeles, primarily African-Americans and Latino Americans lived in the ghetto created by the projects because that is what they could afford. And the ghetto afforded protection and belonging. Why do you think grown men still call their house "the crib"?

As children, the projects were awesome! We played outside all day until the streetlights came on. Sound similar to the suburbs? It was. We played Double Dutch, shot marbles, climbed trees, ate "sweet babies," and on and on. We had community personalities similar to those immortalized in movies: Ms. Paula, she made the best cookies. Mr. Barnard, he sold candy in the community—he and Ms. Paula battled for the affection of the children and the title of Candy Man or Candy Lady—and everyone's friend, the insurance man, Mr. Sikes. The projects were like *The Andy Griffith Show*—in color.

But don't let me fool you. To me, the projects were awesome, they were home; but in reality, they were a beautiful mess. One day we

---

[1] As an aside, there is a 1966 film titled *Fantastic Voyage*, and there's a common theme between all three works of the same title.

would ride bikes and make Kool-Aid popsicles, and the next, a helicopter would fly low, searching for a criminal who just happened to be lying in a pool of blood outside our front door. One night, Grandpa Willie and his band would be outside plucking away, the stringed music and low reverberant sound of voices and water jugs pulsing into the night sky, and the next night shrapnel rap (the kind of rap where the bass is so loud it pierces your ears like shrapnel) would blare, people would make and sling crack pies, and the police sirens would show up. One summer's eve, we would have dance-offs and practice cheers, and the next we would hear my auntie's best friend was dead—her boyfriend had killed her; they fought too much.

I learned to fight for life there. Grandma took us to church, and she often prayed aloud. I understood something radical occurred when she prayed, but I didn't know what. Kids played hide and seek; some played hide and go get it (there was some type of sexual encounter when "it" found someone to "get"). I didn't play that game. My experiences taught me to fight for my life, not to give it away so cheaply—at least while I was young.

Shameka, one of my earliest childhood friends whom I met when I was about six or seven years old, and I would go up to the school to play tetherball. We would take a basketball, two plastic bags, and a long phone cord. We slipped the ball into the bags, tied it up with the phone cord, and played tetherball for hours. The dirt from the ground would rise up and circle around our legs as we jerked back and forth, jockeying for an edge. Loose berets would fly through the air as we hit the ball with a thud and a grunt. Each hit stung survival, each swing batted competition, each loss spoke devastation, for a moment.

Tetherball became a good metaphor for life. The only way to win was to beat the heck out of it, and if I let it get by, in just a few moments it would be strangling the source—out of reach. The harder I hit it, the harder she hit back, but the better chance I had of winning.

The projects behaved like a living, breathing organism. The movement, the beautiful browns and oranges, topazes and purples of the low-riders, some mural painted, hittin' switches, children whizzing past on bikes followed by younger toddlers waddling and falling forward, trying to chase down the older brother or sister, dancing, loving, people coming and going, moving and selling, the outfits, fur-lined coats covering tight dresses above stilettos, white A-shirts creeping down to sagged jeans and Timberlands while arms and chests boasted tattoos and necks supported gold and ears carried diamonds, the smiles, waves, laughter and tears—the projects grew and flourished.

Just like any organism, sometimes regeneration came through death. I don't mean to make light of the situation, but the projects had rules. Sometimes, people broke the rules, and in the projects, the dead leaves fell and became fertilizer for the dirt. I don't agree with the rules of the projects—life is so much more important than rules, yet so fragile it can be taken when we break them—but I do want to paint the picture of the life cycle within the rules of the projects. One part of the life cycle is death; one result of breaking the rules in the projects was death too.

On a night when the temperature rose high and the smog hung low, the police helicopter buzzed lowly overhead. Descending like locusts with torch lights swaying back and forth, back and forth, the helicopter inched ever closer, dauntingly. The pressure cooker inched toward eruption, steam forced itself upward, billowing around the lid, rattling against the sides. Someone had broken the rules, and the situation had grown explosive.

Standing in the doorway, all of five or six years old, I didn't know what was happening, but I could feel the intense pressure and hear the chopper hanging low, sweeping the dust into mini-tornadoes. Through the darkness a man named Bugs came gaping across the lawn. He was stumbling, falling, crawling, reaching. Blood poured from his shirt onto his pants and spilled out onto the sparsely patched lawn—more dust than grass. Bugs looked at me; I should have been in bed, should have been in the house, but I was transfixed by the drama, the interruption in our community.

His eyes rolled toward me, threatening to leap from their orbits and cry out for help. He reached for me. Blood pooled beneath his body, leaving a trail on the grass that glimmered in the lights from the helicopter. A sound barked through the thrust of the spinning blades, cutting through the night sky and roaring engines. "Stop!" a bullhorn demanded, but Bugs continued to crawl. His shirt hung from his body, draping downward, open from a blade slice. He was cut, not stabbed—but sliced.

Crawling slowly toward the door, his stare penetrated mine. He stared right through me, and I turned away in a panicked sweat. The intensity heightened. The bullhorn sounded again, the house shook, and the helicopter inched ever closer. I squeezed my stomach to keep from urinating on myself. It was a pleasant pain because my insides were frenzied, yet I knew I had to hold it in. Bugs reached again, and then collapsed onto the lawn, disappearing behind the door my

Momma had just slammed shut before me. He was gone. But his memory was cut indelibly into my mind.

When I think back about that night, I still see Bugs' eyes in my mind's eye; I still see his blood draining, and I still see his hand reaching, reaching for me. He had broken a rule, not a rule of law, but a rule of the projects. Someone had punished him, and it cost him his life. I still see his hand reaching, reaching for me, asking me to save him.

The more I think about it, the more I am convinced Bugs wasn't reaching for me at all. He was reaching for something more. He was reaching for something beyond his reach, just past his fingertips, something a blink away from his reality. He was reaching for something he couldn't obtain—maybe the same ideal that drove him to break the rule of the projects—something invisible. He was reaching for life. Not his life, no, he was reaching for a life he had never found in the projects, trying to move, and when he reached the wrong way, it cost him.

A leaf that falls from a plant goes through a process of decomposition and provides fertilization for the soil. The seeds germinate and spring up into new life in the fertile soil. If the leaf never dies, new life can't begin. That's the rule of life. I can't figure it out. I know Bugs died and I know he broke the rules, but I don't know what new life he brought. It seems as if he died to keep life the way it was, to protect the life of the projects.

I can still see Bugs, and he haunts me. Most of my memories of Jordan Downs are of childhood delight, and most of them are nostalgic. Not Bugs. He doesn't fit. Even in my memory, he breaks the rules.

In the School House

I was a rule follower. I liked the rules: the straight lines and dos and don'ts. Making people happy by following the rules was part of my persona. In fact, the rules made me happy because rules were guardrails. They were a form of protection and a way to know if I was doing wrong or right. I liked the rules, and that is why I loved school.

One thing I did not love was going to school. I loved school, but I didn't want to *go.* My tantrums waxed colossal, catastrophic, comical. Momma would try to take me to school, and even in Pre-K, I threw tantrums rivaling any famous scold: Tom Walker's wife, Cinderella's sisters, Shakespeare's Katherina (the shrew), Martin Lawrence's Shanae-nae. Kicking, screaming, biting, crying, rolling on the floor, hiding my shoes, all of these were part of my repertoire. Like loose change in the hot clothes dryer, I would clang around, screaming, "I don't wanna go to school! I don't wanna go to school!"

We had a school on site at Jordan Downs. Momma would drop me off at the classroom, and teachers would have to distract me so she could get away. Any excuse I could use, I would try. I'd scream, "Oh, no! I have to give her a kiss. I have to give Momma a kiss," knowing full well I had just kissed her goodbye that morning. When Momma would sneak out, she always had a small smirk on her face. To this day I wonder was she happy someone else had to deal with those tantrums, or did she smirk because she was proud of herself for having a daughter who couldn't let her go? Maybe, I'll ask her someday.

Once inside the school, I loved school! My favorite teacher, Ms. Etherton, was a vortex. Wherever she went, students followed. She had this way about her, something that would draw me in and make me feel important. Have you ever met someone like her? Have you met someone who looked you in the eye and made you feel like you mattered, like you were the only one in the room, like your words were interesting? If you have, then you know that when she spoke, *I* would listen.

I remember one cute lesson she taught me about the difference between an action verb and a state-of-being verb. Now, don't let your eyes roll back in your head and your heart sink when you read grammatical terms. I'm a teacher, but I'm no grammarian. I came from South Central, not South Cambridge.

Me and Ms. Etherton, I mean, *Ms. Etherton and I*, were looking for the scissors, and I spotted them.

"Here they go, Ms. Etherton, here the scissors go!"

"Sweetie, scissors don't have legs; the scissors aren't *going* anywhere."

"Here they *are,* Ms. Etherton, here *are* the scissors."

I don't remember what grade or class she taught, but I remember *her*. And then we moved.

For a short period, when I was seven years old, we moved out of the projects so we could stay with my mother's boyfriend, the monster with the friendly face. The abuse started. In a brushstroke of time, I was broken, hiding, alone, beginning to fade—and then we moved.

Back to Jordan Downs. I was home again, but I was dead inside, broken again. Back to school I went, voiceless, as I wrote before.

I re-immersed myself in school and began learning, post the trauma of the abuse I suffered, after a few months. Maybe the abuse or maybe the way my memory works keeps me from recalling much else about school at that time in my life. The days became a blur. I don't remember much about the school: the teachers, the students, the classrooms, the sights and smells, but I do remember learning. Some people don't remember learning to count—I do. Some don't remember their first trip to the library—I do. Some don't remember their first book, but I remember. I remember how my first library book looked, smelled, and felt in my hand—I loved it.

I got back into the academic swing of things, and I began perceiving the world differently. Little things were very important to me: using chart paper, saying the pledges, singing "This Land Is Your Land." I don't term those memories as "little" because they are insignificant; I term them as "little" because very few people remember learning the words to songs and pledges. They only remember the words, but I remember *learning* the words, and those "little" memories were something positive I could hold. The abuse had torn a hole in my heart, and I continued to search to find my heart a home.

The projects meant protection to me. The school meant discovery and belonging. For example, we went to a Dodgers game on a field trip, I won a bond for a speech I wrote, and I earned all kinds of awards at my elementary school graduation. Except for those short few months, that little experience of living with the monster with the friendly face who chased me for more than half my life, my elementary school experience was grand. Once I got through the front doors.

I am so nostalgic for those days. When I want to remember the first days of school, when I really want to go back, I take a stroll down the ethnic hair aisle in my local grocery store. I know what I am looking for, and I have no intention to purchase it. I just want to smell it. For some people, it is the smell of chalk dust, for others it is paper, glue, erasers, and for others it is the smell of wooden desks and floor wax that reminds them of the first days of school. When I round the corner of the hair aisle, the white lid stares back at me, standing out from all the others surrounding it. I grab the blue, squatty cylinder and I twist open the white lid to the Blue Magic Hair Grease, lift it to my nose, and inhale. *Ahhh.* The first days of school, Jordan Downs, home.

I am so nostalgic for those days, but something still haunts me. After the abuse, after becoming sexually aware, there was another man who made me fear. During recess, I looked outside the gate, and a middle-aged, white man sat in a green Chevy Nova, just staring. I shuddered. His eyes penetrated me. I told the teachers, and eventually an adult headed in his direction, and he drove off. But on other days, he returned and stared.

In spite of the man in the Nova, in spite of the gangs, the noise, the rules, my memories of the projects are still fond. I wish we would have never moved in with the monster with the friendly face outside of the projects, but I can't change the past. I choose to remember the Kool-Aid pops, the cookies, Double Dutch, and tetherball, lots of tetherball. I learned to fight for my life there, to thrive there, to come into my own there, and then we moved.

Moved

"In my Father's house are many rooms. If it were not so, would I have told you that I go to prepare a place for you?" –John 14:2

Student mobility is a problem. Moving for a student disrupts his or her academic learning environment and progress. Sure, sometimes a move is in the student's best interest; however, most educators believe one move will cost a student approximately twenty-five percent of that academic year's growth.

As adults, we may roll our eyes whether the data is empirical or not. We think, *Get over it already. It's just a new school. How hard can it be to go to class, sit, take some notes, and come home? It's not like . . . work.*

And we are wrong! A new job is the best analogy to a new school. Think about it. Think about a time when you changed jobs. I understand that the point—for most of us—of reading a book is to finish the book, but I want you to let yourself remember. Pick a job. Remember leaving the old job? Slow down. Even if it was under terrible circumstances and the sentiment was "Good riddance" rather than "Goodbye," was leaving still somewhat frightful? You probably left the old job to start the new job laden with some level of apprehension. When you started the new job, was it everything you expected? Did you know how to use the stapler, find the bathroom, order supplies, clock in, even what to wear? Did you get the feeling that people were looking at you funny because you were too excited or too quiet? Were you good at your new job immediately, or did you have a learning curve? One time, I couldn't open the freezer door at my new job. No matter how hard I tried, or who showed me, I couldn't do it for the first week. I had to ask for help opening the door!

Multiply that by ten, and that is what a student deals with when she moves to a new school. Where's the bathroom? How many minutes between classes again? Is math upstairs or downstairs? Am I in the right room? What if I forget my locker combination or I try to open the wrong one? Whom do I sit with at lunch? Why do the boys here tuck in the front part of their shirt but not the back? I'd rather hear, "Who ride gansta, Crip?" than deal with that drama again.

Students who move to a different school undergo a tremendous amount of pressure and stress. Add a new family on top, and it is like shaking up a bottle of skunked beer. No wonder Jesus said He was going to *prepare* a place. Heaven wouldn't be heaven if someone just threw a couple of boxes of halos and wings on the floor and said, "Figure it out. You're a big girl."

That's one of the reasons why I am thankful for angels with scars; they bring peace. My stepfather, Otis, was an altogether separate type of man than whom I had met before. He was kind, structured, interested in the arts, mature. He didn't ignore me. He didn't abuse me. He was interested.

Momma met Otis sometime around the end of my elementary school education. We had lived in Jordan Downs, moved in and out of the home of the monster with a friendly face, and moved back to Jordan Downs before they met. My father wavered in and out of the picture, available on his timetable, but more often than not, unavailable. So when we moved again, between elementary and middle school, at least we moved *toward* masculine kindness with Otis as opposed to the earlier chaos of living with the monster.

In the Middle

Otis was the lynchpin of balance in our lives during that time. Because we moved from the projects, we moved away from Grandma and the stability that came with her. We moved from our home; we moved from my school. Otis provided balance, which to us was uncomfortable. I moved from being the oldest child to a middle child. Otis had a few other children—seventeen total. I suppose he took his calling "to be fruitful and multiply" literally. None of his children lived with us, but I still moved to the middle. And then he and Momma had two more together: Otis, their baby boy, and Otisha, their baby girl. Otisha never made it home from the hospital. I often have wondered if her death tore them apart.

At that time, I had my own problems to solve, namely middle school. I attended Drew Magnet Middle School, where the floor wax squeaked underneath our sneakers and the restroom smelled like pine cleaner and lavender. The walkways were clearly marked, the doors remained open, the hallways stood silent, and the banners were hung with pride. Everything was orderly. Even the restrooms—especially the restrooms.

For each class we organized a different folder. The teachers checked our folders daily. We had to be organized. The teachers pushed us. Punctuality was a must, and although I loved the rules, I finally found out, academically, I wasn't as smart as I thought I was. I was just in the middle.

I joined the Cadets and became the battalion commander, joined color guard, attended church, and grew physically. My life developed some structure, and I loved it. I learned to iron, and I crisply pressed my uniforms. The Cadets marching came naturally, and the crisp green grass crunched deliciously beneath my plain black marching shoes. "Left, left, left, right, left, we would call," and I always wanted to be the one to answer.

My school and extra-curricular activities gave me structure, and my teachers gave me inspiration. I have an affinity for spotting great teachers; it's a gift. Since I wasn't always a great student, and I was very aware of the adult presence, I watched teachers scrupulously. Mr. Lattimore was my favorite math teacher, Mr. Traylor my favorite history, Ms. Njoku my favorite science, and Ms. Enberg was my favorite English teacher. All of them taught at Drew Magnet. All of them pushed me. All of them showed interest in me.

And then someone blew the top off. Momma fell in love with a man named Michael, and by "in love," I mean she swooned at the sound of his name. Middle school ended. Middle child status ended. Structure and balance ended, and then we moved.

Under the Bridge

Some people move out from underneath a bridge and into a house. We moved from a house to underneath a bridge. We didn't literally move under a bridge, but to an eighth grader, it felt like it. From the house where we lived with Otis, Momma, and her five kids: myself, Connie Jr., Ieshia, Daron, and Otis Jr. all moved in with her new boyfriend, Michael. I no longer stabilized in the middle; I moved back to being the oldest. I was the oldest of five children in a home sometimes without electricity, running water, and no means of transportation. Life fluctuated more chaotically, but I still had Drew Magnet School until the end of that year. Then the riots began.

Before my ninth-grade graduation, riots broke out in L.A. Violence surrounded the famous court case where a man, Rodney King, was the focal point. Police arrested King after he attempted to evade the police in a high-speed chase. What brought so much attention to the case was the way they arrested King. He seemed to resist, and they beat him mercilessly for it. Someone captured the entire incident on camera. Another problem painted itself vibrantly across the videotape: King was black, and the four officers who hit him more than fifty times were white.

Thus began the media frenzy and the civil unrest. At the time, several claims of police brutality existed in L.A., the city smoldered uneasily, and the video footage pushed people to the ledge. The media had their story, civil rights activists had ammunition for their cause, and the African-American community had their proof. King should have never led the police on a crazy high-speed chase. The police should have never treated a man, any man, the way they did Rodney that day. Something needed to be done, but when the police were acquitted of the crime, the city exploded. Everyone jumped off the ledge.

People rioted in the streets. Some burnt cars and buildings, some rioted against the police, and some robbed the city businesses blind. Some say, "Cheaters gonna cheat!" I say, "Looters gonna loot!" And loot they did, to the tune of hundreds of millions of dollars. The paradox was the riots stood for a rallying cry against the inappropriate treatment of black people by white police officers; instead, it turned into black people destroying other black people's homes, neighborhoods, and businesses. Chaos ruled my city and my life; I didn't walk to school those days. And then I moved.

In the Moment

I learned to live in the moment. I walked slowly, entering Washington Magnet High School as a sophomore, and I broadcasted naivety and greenness. My family didn't move physically, but I moved from junior high to high school. The summer before, I took some summer school classes to prepare me for high school—I had fallen behind academically. I still wasn't prepared. Drew Magnet School had been my palace of peace during the chaos of my life in middle school. Some kids experimented with alcohol, drugs, and sex, often during school, but not me. I was green, but safe, yet now I left the middle school and walked into a new situation.

I avoided compromising situations because of my past abuse, and my body tried to hide itself too. As a freshman, I weighed less than ninety pounds, and I hadn't hit puberty. My uniform helped me fit in. Washington was a preparatory school, so we had to wear uniforms, which fit me just fine. My uniform helped me hide in the crowd, but I didn't actually fit. I didn't fit, and then we moved.

I moved from Washington Magnet High School to San Bernardino High, my second high school in 1992. At San Bernardino, I dove in heartfirst. For example, in English class, I devoured *A Tale of Two Cities* by Charles Dickens. I could relate. The dichotomy, the bipolarity of living in two different worlds—one in my head and one at my house, one in my school and one in my broken heart—resonated within me. The superlatives "best" and "worst" in the opening lines described my hypersensitivity and confusion—I believed I was a little bit of both. Everything was extreme.

I am an overcomer, and I know if you are reading this book, you are one too. I chose to make it the best of times. I tried out for the football team—as a girl. I joined the creative writing club with the belief I could make a difference. I studied literature to gain wisdom, I searched for God to find hope and light, and although we lived on food stamps and I placed cardboard in my shoes to protect my feet from the holes worn through the soles, I still believed I had everything before me. And then we moved.

I can't remember walking through the doors of my third high school in that year-and-a-half period, Crenshaw High School. The experience of *new* grew old. I don't even remember if I made any friends that year. I do remember that my obstacles were my preparation to overcome, and my setbacks were my setup to make a difference. By now I was immune to moving. The moving had taken its toll, but I kept moving forward. I joined the thematic and dramatic club, performed poetry out loud, and entered competitions where I recited poetry by Ntozake Shange. I spent as much time as possible with my Grandpa, at school and at church, and then we moved.

In His Arms

In 1994, I started my fourth and final high school, Fremont High. School wasn't hard for me at this time, but I had lost all of my structure, all continuity. I remember cheating on a French test and the teacher caught me. She graciously gave me another opportunity, and when I studied and actually took the test, I aced it. I possessed the talent, but my heart was not in it. The structure was missing.

Before long, a green car eerily rolled up. A green station wagon began following me to and from school. My nightmare, a reminder of the green Nova from my childhood, was chasing me. I wanted to go home, back to the projects, back to the little girl before the abuse. Who was this man, and why was he following me? I walked on.

During this time, I met Zeus and No Name, and some other guys. As often happens with young girls, my heart strained for something, and since it wandered from school and the future, my heart turned to young boys. As a response to my past abuse, I had successfully avoided sexual encounters until this time. Slowly, I gave in. I compromised myself and grew further detached. The innate ability I fostered as a child, the ability to detach during sexual abuse for the sake of survival, became my drug as a late teenager. Sex produced the means to get physical affection from a man without giving him my heart. I wonder.

Eventually, I fell into the arms of another man. I had moved so much, I needed someone to move me. As I sit here now, I can vaguely remember the melody to a song, wandering up behind me, quietly, softly, calmly breezing by my ear, "Move in a way that I've never seen before / Cause there's a mountain in the way and a lock on the door / I'm drifting away, waves are crashing on the shore / So, Lord, move, or move me" (Deibler).

I needed someone to move me because the green station wagon reminded me of what was behind, and I had no idea what was ahead. I wanted to go to college, be a teacher, or lawyer, or police officer, yet I didn't know how. Never did I know my abuse from my past would show up in my future and wreck me.

Abuse

"Why did I come out from the womb to see toil and sorrow, and spend my days in shame?"–Jeremiah 20:18

On a beautiful summer day in 1984, I remember looking at the heart of a dandelion, flecked with a dark obsidian color, emboldened by the radiant yellow and porous appearance of the heart. I rubbed the yellow off on my arm and let the dandelion head fall listlessly into the thick, green grass at my feet. My robin-egg-blue dress shoes strapped over tiny, white socks contrasted brilliantly with the dark smoothness of my skin and blurred softly into a trail of white echo, as I swung my feet back and forth joyfully. I was a small child, sitting on a lopsided, wooden folding chair in the cemetery. To me, the day promised perfection and playtime in the park. For the others, the day promised dreariness; dreariness resided in their hearts because they had lost a brother. I remember the preacher, loud and booming, repetitively raising his eyebrows and cocking his head backward when he raised his voice. His intense eyes scanned the crowd as he eulogized the man whose body begged to be laid to rest in the ground.

And then something remarkable happened. A middle-aged, black woman walked up to the podium in the middle of a perfunctory, lifeless service on the lawn of a forever-green cemetery, while the June breeze blew, and delivered a brutal elegy. Oh, how I have searched and searched and finally found it, an age-old elegy previously recorded. Since I have discovered it, I can share it here, and so it reads:

"Severed"

The heart was pumping;
The artery clamped, then severed,
And you were severed from reality,
And we were severed from peace,
And our hearts stopped beating.

When the flow of blood stopped;
The blood dried and clotted,
And you were severed from life,
And we were severed from hope,
And our hope stopped beating.

Now you're severed from our embrace;
The casket buried in dirt,
And you will be eaten by worms,
And we will be eaten by pain,
And our lives stopped meaning.

The imagery of the elegy shocked us, and the message of the poet infuriated us, so hopeless, so punctuated by self-absorption. I hated the poet. Who writes of the desperate loss of a loved one with only her feelings in mind? Who focuses only on herself and does not focus on memorializing the lost loved one?

The victim of abuse does.

The story is a lie. No cemetery, no green grass and yellow dandelion, no white socks with blue shoes, and no preacher with enlarged eyes were present. Only loss and pain. The victim buried was I, the innocent girl before the abuse. The author of the elegy was I, the shattered girl left behind. I was a walking contradiction—one foot in the grave and one foot out. I wasn't self-absorbed; I was the walking dead, the body left behind. Left behind in June of 1984, and again, and again.

What follows is a history of my sexual abuse. As you can tell, I have alluded to it many times previously, but I haven't directly recorded what happened. I have been avoiding it. In the face of danger, we often shrink back, fear others' perceptions and judgments, hope for an easy way out, and pray we do not come face to face with our tormentors. I have been avoiding it because to write about it is to immortalize it, to display it is to put it in the spotlight. However, to hide it is to allow it to remain in the darkness, seething, searching for other victims to oppress and smother. I have been avoiding it because it causes painful memories for me and for other victims as well as for the perpetrators. I have been avoiding it because—as awful as this sounds—it stimulates some and breaks others. I have known men and women who have had to put down a book or quit watching a movie that sensationalized sexual abuse. I hate sexual abuse, but I don't want my story to cause hate. I'll let God be the judge of the people; I'll tell you about the abuse.

I share my abuse to equip some to overcome their past, to beg others to stop their behavior, and to urge all to watch, protect themselves and their children, and to promote freedom. I hope from reading my story you are emboldened to protect others and freed to share your story.

As a disclaimer, this will be graphic. At any time, if you cannot continue, feel free to skip to the next chapter. For those of you who continue to read, we are going to start with answering the question: What did I do wrong?

What Did I Do Wrong?

"Cursed be the day on which I was born!"–Jeremiah 20:14

What did I do wrong?

I was born.

The sound of his feet shuffling across the floor sent a cold, merciless anxiety into my stomach. I would start to cry then, at the sound of his calloused feet scraping across the linoleum floor, edging toward my door. I couldn't hide, I couldn't escape, and the monster approached. He didn't come from the closet, nor untuck himself from under the bed. He slowly traipsed in from my Momma's bedroom.

He reached down and grabbed me by the arm, lifted me from the floor, placed his thumb in the dimple underneath my deltoid and pushed. I writhed and wiggled, but I muffled my own screams—the fear in me was greater than the pain without. *What would he do to*

Momma? The fear monster was home. He dragged me quietly into the bathroom and smiled. My tears fell to the floor in masses, streams running down my cheeks, sobs escaping from the corners of my mouth.

He put a stop to that. He unzipped his blue jeans and inserted his penis in my mouth. No more annoying sobbing for him. My little body rocked back and forth, tears falling like rivulets, and I prayed for God to kill me. The floor creaked under my knees; I tried to keep quiet. Heat began to rise in me and sweat clung to my body and rolled from my forehead into the tracks laid by my tears. My chest was on fire and my stomach knotted. I had so much hate. I hated myself so much. I wanted to stop him. I wanted to stop him.

He stopped himself. His pelvic revolutions stopped, and I saw his clenched body. Then he ejaculated on my face. The unworthy monster showed up. I was alone. Although he stood there, I was alone, and he had used me like a dirty towel. I would have preferred he urinated on me. *What did I do wrong? What did I do wrong to make him do this to me?* I remember the smell, like chalk, or sweat, or sulfur, or damnation as I wiped my face.

He left. My tears dried up as I stared hard at the little girl in the mirror. I was seven years old, and I hated the face looking back at me. She deserved to die. No more tears. No more pain. The room faded to blue, then gray, then black, and the girl inside me died. We didn't have a funeral or a casket, only a dead body and a shell.

Whom Did I Tell?

Nobody. At first, I didn't tell anybody. I didn't have the words, I didn't know how, I was voiceless. Then, I told everybody. I told them through my actions, and I told them through my words, but nobody listened. They could hear the noise, but they couldn't hear *me*.

Tantrums are one of the first signs something is wrong with a child. Of course, children throw tantrums over small, insignificant issues, so all tantrums do not indicate a hurt deeper than selfishness; some tantrums are displays of misbehavior over issues that are meaningless to adults. But to kids, the issues are monumental. The tough part about parenting is deciphering when a child is throwing a tantrum because he or she can't handle disappointment or if the behavior is inappropriate due to inappropriate behavior. That idea is worth repeating in the form of a question: Is the behavior inappropriate due to other inappropriate behavior?

In my situation, I had rage. My tiny, black knuckles turned white hot as I clung on to anything that felt like security. At other times, the rage turned my hands into fists. Abuse created metamorphosis, and baby hands of caring and trust mutated into weapons. And the tantrums raged. Previously, I had had tantrums about going to school, but these became more colossal, increasingly monumental tantrums. My entire body tensed up, my teeth clenched, I shook, almost imperceptibly at first, but then I flailed into a full-body convulsion. I beat my head against the wall, my fists against the floor, and kicked anything in sight while I screamed. Screaming was a mechanism to let out the rage, and screams flooded out of me like torrents of water from a loosened fire hydrant. My mother was beside herself.

"Shree! What the hell is wrong wit' you! You acting like a lunatic!"

And I would cry, and cry, and cry.

"I want to talk to Grandma! I want to call Grandma! I want to talk to Grandma!"

Silence. The dialing mechanism on the rotary phone spun softly back into place, making a distinct *click*, before the next dial brought some solace to my tormented soul as I stared wildly at Momma with bulging eyes and palpable fear draped on my face.

"Grandma? Hello?"

"What's wrong, baby?"

"Grandma, I love you. Grandma, I love you. I need to see you! Can you come get me? I love you! I need to see you! Come get me, come get me, come get me, come get me . . ."

And she would. Momma thought I was hysterical, but the hysterics were real. I wasn't schizophrenic or bipolar; I was a soda bottle filled with Mentos, shaken, tamped tight—ready to explode.

And then we moved. We moved back in with Grandma. Back to Jordan Downs, back home . . . but he followed me. He chased me through my memories, lurking in my dreams. He peered from behind the curtains, snickered in the closet, and moaned under the bed. He spoke to me in my daydreams, and he whispered in the restroom. The bathtub was my nightmare—each moment filled with panic, imagining the door creaking open, his body entering with wild, crazy eyes peering down from a soulless face. He followed me. He followed me. He followed me to my Auntie Bailey's.

Momma didn't know. My behavior grew wild and reckless, and her "What's wrong, child?" never solicited a true answer, only a question: *What's wrong with me that made him do this?* And then it happened again.

The breathing was heavy. Everyone was asleep at my Auntie's house except me. Inhale, exhale, soft snore, hold your breath, deep tremors. He was there. Momma fell asleep on a pallet on the floor, and he lay next to her; it wasn't a daydream or a whisper this time, he was there. I pretended to sleep near the bottom of the pallet, but it was an act. Like a possum, I played dead—a defense mechanism to ward off predators and make the prey seem undesirable. But human predators believe "playing dead" to be consent, an invitation even, so he began to caress me. Momma was only inches away, asleep, and I kept looking up at her, pleading with her to wake up with my eyes, but I never made a sound.

His hand ran down my body, under my nightgown, and to my panties. A blunt instrument, the hand was rough and harsh and brought tears to my eyes. My eyebrows furrowed, face wrinkled, my eyes scrunched as tightly as I could hold them. My legs stiffened. I lay lifeless: like a board, petrified, calloused in return, wishing for escape. This time I wouldn't perform, and in my mind, I begged, *Please don't! Please don't! Please don't!*

Tears. Fatigue. Hopelessness. Giving in. Numb. Dead. I disconnected from reality the only way a child can, I shut down my senses and imagined; I imagined I were dead.

When he stopped, I didn't move, didn't breathe, didn't want to attract any more attention. The tears still grew puddles beside my face, but I brought no attention to my existence. I didn't sleep that night, but I played dead through another nightmare.

Did Anyone Find Out?

Thanatosis they call it, toxic immobility, "playing dead." At night, I played dead, and during the day, I became the nightmare. As I already indicated, tantrums may be a sign of abuse, as is restlessness, sleeplessness, weariness, violence, night terrors, and other such erratic behaviors. These behaviors are not to be ignored. When I began grabbing at my own flesh and trying to tear it away, when I began kicking cabinet doors violently, when I began crying uncontrollably, when I began staring blankly into the nothingness on the other side of my eyeballs, I began crying for help. Nobody heard me. Playing dead didn't help. Wreaking havoc didn't help. So I listened for help.

Momma was a kitchitician. Now, if you don't know what a kitchitician is, you've been underprivileged. A kitchitician is a beautician who does hair in the kitchen. That's what Momma did. Often in the summer or when I stayed home from school, Momma would be cutting, braiding, ironing, or weaving hair in the kitchen while I played under the table. The women would gossip back and forth, commenting about how good-for-nothin' their men were, about how bratty their children were, and about themselves and how "bomb" they were; but a sense of pride was always in their voices, pride in their menfolk, pride in their children, feigned pride in themselves.

One afternoon, while the sun beamed down through the window and stole the shade from under the table, I heard Momma "Uh-huh" deeply as she swiftly braided another strand of her friend's hair.

"Can you believe Brandy? She didn't know? She didn't know her man was touchin' those kids? *Sure*, she didn't know. She's too busy with a steady stream of men coming in and out her be'room ta know. She be steady changin' men. Gets her floors waxed by a new fella mor'n I get my hair done!"

Momma said, "Girl, you don't know she ain't watchin' em kids! C'mon now, she didn't know."

"You don't think they tried to tell her? *Naw*, she didn't listen—too worried 'bout her men to notice!"

"I don't know."

"I tell you this, my kids better tell me if *anyone* be tryin' to touch them."

"Girl, you got that right," Momma said, "My kids know they can tell me if anyone tries to lay a finger on 'em."

"Uhum."

Then I knew. Momma had opened the door for me to come tell her. She opened the door by allowing me to stay in the kitchen while she worked. She opened the door by having conversations in front of me, and she opened the door by letting out her true feelings. Momma didn't know it at the time, but she was being vulnerable right there in front of me. The light shined a little brighter under the table, my safe-haven, and chased away more darkness than had been chased in months.

I went to my Auntie Bailey's house that weekend, reluctantly. A few weeks after the molestation started, terror kept me from spending the night at other peoples' homes, or even leaving my home for a day. After I was fondled at my Auntie's home, fear chased me everywhere. The weekend after I had heard Momma say I could tell her anything, I chose to leave the house with my newfound confidence . . . but I didn't stay gone for long.

I called Momma—I feared telling her face to face, not because of real fear, but childhood fear of confrontation—and I told her about the abuse. I told of the touching and the threats, the lies and the abuse, the bathroom floor and the night at Auntie Bailey's, and the calloused, calloused hands, feet, and heart.

Momma told Grandma. Grandma told God and the doctor—and who knows who else. I remember riding in the car with my head against the window, watching the concrete sidewalks and streetlights pass by as we headed to the healthcare clinic, Watts Clinic, on 103rd street. I remember speaking with the doctor, but I don't remember what I said. I remember arriving at Bebe's—she was a lady my Grandma knew from church who would pray over me—and Bebe put her hands on my shoulders and head and prayed for me in another language. Grandma said she was speaking in tongues. I remember being able to breathe, for the first time in years, as if a large balloon taking up my entire chest had been deflated.

The terrors, tremors, and tantrums began to disappear; however, the rage remained. I thought I had taken it all out on the tetherball and beaten it down, down, down, but it remained within me. The rage surfaced through my passivity, my ability to disconnect, my inability to say no. Every time some evil came my way, I accepted it. Oh, I tried to avoid it, but when the evil arrived, I disconnected, played dead, tried to survive, and the abuse followed me.

How Did I Get Here?

How did I get here? In a green Chevy Nova. The Nova represents the voyage, my abduction, my abuse; it brings continuity to the feelings of helplessness from the first time I heard the calloused feet, to the last inappropriate touch, and it creates an image of being followed, watched, and stalked by a mercenary of my youth—for my soul. The Chevy Nova represents the day innocence transmuted into fear, and love changed to hate. A few years later, while we lived with Otis and the swinging tetherball swung as a beaten piece of nostalgia, I went for a ride in the Chevy Nova. Right across the street.

My neighbor, also a preteen black girl, with whom I felt comfortable, invited me to sleep over. With her, I had experienced the freedom to feel at ease with a friend; I didn't need to look over my shoulder, and I decided to have fun at her house.

I let myself go. The afternoon blurred into evening, watching television, playing with dolls—even though I didn't really like dolls—and eating dinner. Her living room offered comfort, lying on the floor, watching television and eating popcorn felt perfectly natural, inviting even. Life at her house felt better than normal. Her parents seemed better than normal; they respected each other—no fighting—and treated each other kindly—no red flags. She actually had a father in the home, and he didn't seem to have any intention of touching me. I let my guard down.

As we lay in bed that night, a familiar, eerie feeling climbed up my spine and wrapped itself around my throat. My body sensed something unsettling, something causing me fear, but I didn't know what it was. I started to breathe heavily, to pant, and almost hyperventilate. I knew I needed to go home. I looked at the door, for the shadows, the feet, the fear, but nothing moved. And then it happened.

She climbed on top of me. She pushed her face down on top of mine, hard, and kissed my face, hard. I wanted to scratch out her eyeballs and yank out all of her hair, but I froze. The perpetrator always sees inaction as consent. No matter what, even if you beg, the perpetrator always sees inaction as consent. I asked her to stop. I tried to push her away, but because I didn't kick her, or bite her, or scream, she continued. I cried, bit my tongue, thought, *Oh, God, what did I do wrong, how did I get here again?* Then I disconnected my mind from my body.

She put her head between my legs, and my body froze from my eyeballs to my toes—determined not to react, not to feel. My feelings numbed and my eyes rolled back to make room for the tears while my brain turned my vision into a thick, gray fog. I felt nothing. I remembered nothing. I was a corpse once again. I went home in the morning, foggy and mutilated, walking, walking, walking as I would continue to do for many years. Walking to clear my head, walking to get me places, walking to get away. *No more rides in the Nova,* I thought. *I will protect myself from now on.*

Why is He a Part of Me?

All the moving started: and then we moved, and then we moved, and then we moved . . . Momma's boyfriends came and went, we left Otis, Michael, and others behind. I escaped. I escaped the childhood monster, the neighbor with the friendly face but nefarious intentions, and the green Chevy Nova. I escaped my absent father, my calloused mother, and nestled into the arms of the only man who had remained faithful my whole life, my grandfather Hosea. He was the one man in my life I could trust.

Hosea was a kind man with a sordid past. He spent fifteen years in jail for a violent crime, but the felon was never the man I knew. The man I knew was Momma's daddy, Grandma's husband, and he made me comfortable with myself. Born in Arkansas in the 1940s, Papaw was not a stranger to mistreatment. He grew up in poverty and learned to make a living on his own labor and wit despite his youth. His mind remained a steel trap; he didn't have the academics people often associate with being intelligent, but he had something else. He knew things. And he knew how to *do* things.

Often, Papaw could be found under the hood of a neighbor's car, repairing window air conditioners in a neighbor's home, or replacing a water line in a neighbor's backyard. He spoke easily and generously, and for that, he always seemed to gather a crowd. His stories ended with laughter, and his audience, whether one or many, left with a desire for more. His presence often seemed insatiable.

Somewhere inside was a dark side to Papaw, a deep, hidden-away secret with reticent fears and desires, but we never knew where. His daughter, my mother, was the only one of his children to live with him. Two other daughters, both younger, lived with his sister. I never understood why. The story *went* he and Grandma were too impoverished to raise all three of their daughters together, but it never held water. Papaw was a man of a sharp mind and creative hands—a salt-of-the-earth type—and those men never wanted for work to do. And when a valuable man works, he eats, and so does his family. No, I didn't believe it. Another story loomed behind those blue eyes and wavy hair. My light-skinned, gregarious Papaw had some skeletons in the closet.

Despite the skeletons, Papaw lived by the work of his hands, and he took a hands-on approach to everything. He made time to work with those he loved. He often made me trinkets and keepsakes based on what I liked. I remember one time visiting a jewelry store and a necklace hung in the display case connected by three gold strands: yellow, rose, and white. He saw me eyeing the necklace, but I walked out of the store without it—I couldn't afford it. The next time I went to his home, my necklace waited for me, a gift from my Papaw.

I spent hours after school at Papaw's house. Papaw was a leaky faucet. Most of us associate a dripping, leaky faucet with a nuisance beyond compare. The infernal dripping and splashing of one lone drop of water will infuriate even the most docile of men. But Papaw was a good leaky faucet. Slowly, methodically, he dripped wise sayings or small tears of knowledge for me to soak up. When we worked on my animal projects for science, he seemed to know everything about livestock, but he didn't brag. He allowed the drips to fall, saturate, and be absorbed before he dropped another one.

Spending the days at his house was therapeutic. The home was comfortable and inviting and our conversations ran long and deep. We discussed politics, literature, relationships, and theories. He helped me with my schoolwork, and he talked with me about boys. We even talked about the birds and the bees. The only thing we didn't talk about was his past.

One evening, while we built a puzzle like we often did, and watched figure skating on television, we maintained a light, arid, and playful back-and-forth banter typical of our evenings together during my sophomore year of high school. I lay on my side, placing another piece in the puzzle, looking up at the television, when everything stopped. He placed his hand on my right breast and stroked. Then he began to squeeze it, fondle it, and hold it.

I saw no movement on the television, heard no sound, felt no pain, only the lonely rubbing of one hand on my right breast. I did not comprehend. As quickly as it started, it stopped, and he sat back like nothing changed. But my whole perception of him changed in one dark moment, yet he sat and went back to piecing together the puzzle. For a moment, I stared blindly, found my voice, and then said, "Papaw, I didn't like that."

He responded, "Oh, I'm sorry," and kept putting together the puzzle. The paradigm shifted. My assailant was now part of my family, part of me. I came from the same man who only moments before tried to destroy me. *Was the monster inside of me too?*

I stopped going to my Papaw's house. The visits grew less frequent, and the duration of my sleep grew more and more. Less time in relationship, more time in my head and in my bed. With my best relationship severed, with no one to trust, loneliness set in. I sought refuge in sexual misconduct. My body had always been small and petite; however, throughout my high school years I developed very large breasts, and I decided if they were going to be used, they were going to be used at my command and for my control. One broken relationship led to many more broken relationships and crushed my relationship capacity to death.

After high school graduation, I received a gift from my Papaw. I believe it was a peace offering—a declaration of his love for me, an apology for his mistreatment of my body, and an heirloom because he was dying. Shortly thereafter, cancer snatched the life out of him, quickly, deftly, leaving the rest of us nearly unawares. Papaw never saw me visit him while he was sick; he died without my being near. I like to believe his mind had already been impacted by the cancer when he touched me inappropriately, but I never knew—we never discussed it. We never said goodbye.

On the day of the funeral, I walked into the funeral home and paid my respects as did the rest of the family. Nobody else knew the secret at that time, but me. I marched to his casket, but I couldn't bring myself to touch his hands. When I looked down on his frail body in the casket, I shed one tear for him, one last drop from the faucet, and then I turned, walked briskly away, and passed out on the floor.

Why Does He Keep Chasing Me?

I walked everywhere. Walking, a continual motion of feet treading on pavement and legs stretching forward, hips rotating, arms swinging first forward then back, a steady progress toward a destiny. Walking was a source of comfort as much as it was a means of transportation—breathing, thinking, seeing were all a part of the experience that cleansed me, hurried me away from trouble, and kept me moving forward. I walked to football games, school, and the store. I came home from late-night journalism and creative writing classes, student council, athletic training, and many other activities by walking. Walking was a way of life, and it never failed me, lied to me, or used me. When I walked, I was in control.

One late, autumn night when the wind blew hotly down the street and around the corners in gusts, I walked home near dusk. I attended Fremont High School at the time and stayed out late because journalism club ran over and I walked the long walk home. The streetlights buzzed on and the car headlights began to illuminate the sidewalks and reflect through the chain-link fences, casting crisscross shadows on the grass. I walked with the flow of traffic and noticed my shadow in front of me on the sidewalk, mimicking my steps. I turned, but the car behind me drove past, innocuous, unnoticeable, forgettable. What came next wasn't. I stepped into my driveway and pushed open the gate when I heard the rev of an engine. I whirled to close the gate only in time to see this green station wagon barrel in behind me. The driver pulled up sideways, with the rear of his station wagon almost hanging out in the street. I started to panic.

My mind flashed back to elementary school and the green Chevy Nova with the light-skinned man and his piercing eyes, his penetrating stare, and his sneer as he drove away after being chased off by a teacher or administrator. For a moment, I froze. Lost in the shock of fear, I stared, my eyes readjusting from the glare off the headlights. Halos floated and dissolved, my vision started to clear, and I reached for the gate. Out of the car stepped a giant of a man, he was 6'2" or 6'3", and light-skinned. He may have been white or he may have been Latino, but he had dark curly hair, dark eyes, and he was completely naked.

I stared angrily into his eyes, but he looked down at himself to emphasize he was fully primed for action. My wheels began to turn, and I quickly ran toward the door, bolted into the house, and shouted for Momma and Memphis. Memphis grabbed a pistol and ran out into the street wildly. He hustled over to the neighbors' houses and asked them to be on the lookout, but nobody spotted the man in the green station wagon.

Why? Why do men do this? Why do some men think women are longing to stare at their penises, as if that were the most attractive part of a man? Why do they believe this will do something for them? Is there a thrill in seeing a young girl turn away with disgust and fear, and then watching her run away?

What did I do? What did I do to convince people to believe they could touch me? What did I do wrong to entice them? What made him expose himself to me? What did I do wrong?

As evil as my childhood sexual abuse was, the exhibition proved equally evil. I now have a memory stamped into my brain that I never wanted. One I loathe. My eyes were not meant to see him. Instantly, they rejected the sight, but the memory remains, indelibly branded into my mind and upon my thoughts. Maybe he just wanted to be remembered, he and his little, green station wagon.

He showed up again two days later in broad daylight. Again, I was walking—my harmonious detachment from the world now interrupted by one man's Neanderthal behavior—on my way home from school. *Evil bastard!* I thought, but quickly reprimanded myself: one for letting him control and interrupt my memories, and also for cursing him again in my mind. I gazed across the street and beneath the shadow of a storefront awning sat the green station wagon holding the spectacle of my misery. He was watching me.

Now, this happened in a day before everyone owned mobile phones. Most people didn't even have a pager, and surely a poor black girl in L.A. didn't carry one, but I did have quick wits—that day. I didn't freeze this time, but I also didn't run. I walked. I walked it out, just as cool as a cucumber, knowing full well I couldn't run or escape. With one eye on the green station wagon and one eye before me, I walked right on, right into a telephone booth, and I picked up the phone. I put an imaginary quarter, and maybe even a dime, into the slot but kept my eyes on him. I spoke as if I were talking about him, describing him to a friend or to the police, while I stood, arms crossed, staring through the glass of the phone booth, directly at him. He drove away, slowly, looking back over his shoulder as I kept staring. I saw no face as he drove away, no expression, but I imagined he looked disappointed, or incredulous, or crazed, or desperate. I stepped out of the phone booth, clearly the victor, and sprinted home as fast as I could, green station wagons chasing me in my mind.

Why, Dirty Hands? Why?

My heart developed callouses to physical touch. As I became sexually active, intimacy wasn't even a factor, neither was sexual pleasure. In my mind, I surrendered to the belief I was made for this: I was put here for people to put their dirty hands on me and to use me for their own pleasure. My own hands malfunctioned into extensions of my rage. Hands became beings of their own, estranged from hearts and compassion and trust, beings that were meant to destroy, like in a harsh fondle, or hurt like in a clenched fist. If I were put here to be the object that hands controlled, then I was going to control which hands touched me, and they would no longer be dirty hands.

My sexual experiences were disingenuous, offerings of my body on the altar of another man's pleasure, a resolute rejection of God. I needed a Father or a brother to protect me, and I had neither—only dirty hands.

So I used my feet and continued walking. You would think I would have learned to walk facing traffic after my incident with the green wagon twice, but I didn't. On another long trek from school to home, I walked up to a corner where a car sat at a light, running. The driver intended to turn right when the arrow flashed green, but in the meantime, he enjoyed masturbating himself in the comfort of his car. He looked in his mid-fifties, a black man, with no shame. Desensitized thoroughly, I just rolled my eyes, huffed and sighed, and walked on . . . wondering, *What did I do wrong this time?*

What did I do wrong? Why was I molested, touched, treated so harshly by hands?

Nothing. I did nothing wrong. I was born. Not even being born a female, just born. Sexual abuse is not provoked by the victim. Baby diapers aren't too attractive, little boys aren't too stimulating, the incapacitated aren't too tantalizing, and grown women with great figures are not "asking for it." Sexual abuse screams power. The abuser controls the victim's experiences through the use of power—and uses dirty hands to destroy.

Those dirty, dirty hands. All the hands were dirty; I couldn't escape, green cars chased me, memories haunted me, men pursued me, and I always felt fondled by dirty, dirty hands. No pain is quite like the pain one feels when she hates the entire human race—nobody to trust, nobody to love, no reason to live. I didn't truly hate the whole race, but I hated hands, and there was no escaping them. Sometimes, I would wish. I would wish for a pair of clean hands, or maybe just one hand to hold, a hand I could trust to protect me, that didn't want anything from me. Instead, I only found more dirty, dirty hands.

If only I had been holding the nail-pierced ones.

I am not so silly or naïve to suggest if I had been "holding on to Jesus" none of these evil intrusions into my life would have violated me—hardly that. The first followers of Jesus were beaten, burned, crucified, impaled, fed to lions, raped, murdered, and molested. If I had been holding those hands, I may not have escaped the evil of the day, in fact, the evil may have chased me more desperately, but I would have been delivered from the pain of my own destructive choices. My choices with my body would have been different. His hands might have guided me through my next crisis; I may have made different choices.

Paralysis

"Sometimes I think the human heart is just a simple shelf. There is only so much you can pile onto it before something falls off an edge and you are left to pick up the pieces."–Jodi Picoult

In 1993, Nirvana, an alternative rock band with uncanny popularity, released an album that contained a song titled "Rape Me." The song had captured radio time and had been performed live, but now it was crystallized onto CD and released for the masses. And there was an uproar. At first the uproar was subtle, but it gathered steam over time, growing into a more sophisticated response to the edgy title and lyrics. People claimed the song propagated a type of anti-rape anthem, but several misunderstood the true meaning. With harsh, discordant sounds and lyrics, the song intended to epitomize the angry response of the victim—a battle cry of the yet undefeated.

Maybe the song helped. Maybe another teen daughter spoke with her mother or father about rape. Maybe another mom had a tough conversation with her daughter about how to avoid predators. Maybe it saved a few. Maybe.

After moving to Texas to see No Name, I lived with my cousin Sheila, in her garage. I was out of a job, school, and I felt like I lived on skid row. My dreams never materialized and depression crept in. I kept my appearances up, and I worked on finding another job. I garnered a few leads, and I even secured an interview with a lady for a paralegal position. But it did not go well.

I got another lead, and this one looked promising. When I scoped out the position, the data entry job, it appeared to be more of a "high-profile" position, extraordinary for entry-level work, maybe even one that came with a company car. A nineteen-year-old can dream, can't she? I celebrated the interview with No Name, and we yukked it up as I would shortly be a professional woman rolling around in a Jaguar taking clients to and from exclusive destinations. Until then, I had to take the bus or ride with friends.

The morning of the interview, I wanted to look extremely professional, so I put on a starched, button-down shirt, ironed twice to remove any possible trace of a wrinkle, a black skirt, and heels. At nineteen, I appeared very slim and very professional looking. I kept myself as businesslike as possible, and I asked Sheila to take me to the interview. The first red flag, or in my case "green car," should have been arriving in a residential neighborhood for a job interview. I ignored the signs, told Sheila the location was fine, chased my need for validation through career and success, and hustled inside to meet the boss in his duplex condo.

He made the job appear very legitimate, and it might well have been, but I never fully found out. I only stayed long enough to fill out the application, finish the interview, and have Sheila pick me back up. Although he was a middle-aged, white man with dirty fingernails, and we interviewed in his residence, the job seemed very real. He had clients—the office had to be mobile in order to meet the demands of the clients. He didn't work from his home, he only used it for interviewing purposes. He met his clients at mutually agreed upon meeting places. My job required me to organize and keep up with all the paperwork: financial, client-related, service-related, contracts, etc.

The next day, I got up early, donned a very similar outfit—this time the shirt had pinstripes—and I caught the bus to the stop nearest his house. He had awarded me the position near the end of the interview the day before, and in my exuberance, I didn't take much time to process everything we discussed. One item he had made abundantly clear:

I would have to deal with some unfamiliar situations due to his high-profile clients.

This expectation created no issue for me; I liked successful, entertainer types. We were, after all, living in L.A. I walked from the bus stop to his home, to his car, to his trap. We left his home together and headed to meet with his first client. We arrived at a local, happening place called Splash, which boasted a very cosmopolitan, high-end, progressive atmosphere. Although Splash housed an aquatic playland, it was no place for children. Massages, hot tubs, beauty bars, and steam rooms all surrounded the front desk area. People came to Splash for two reasons: to relax and be pampered, or in our case, to impress clients.

He led me through the front doors, and I followed, blindly, the light from the sun gleaming off the glass doors. The lady manning the intake counter smiled nicely, cordially took down our information, and innocently asked if we had bathing suits. Women's intuition flared through my body to the hair on the back of my neck, shocking it up like a defensive feral feline's. I started to back away a bit, but my boss spoke only of the meeting with the clients, his demeanor professional, his voice coaxing and hypnotic. To both the lady in charge of guest reception and to me his voice betrayed no emotion, other than a deep desire to exceed the expectations of his clients. The clients chose Splash for the relaxation—we were accommodating them.

We walked back to the brightly-colored, coral lounge room and sat down to wait on the clients privately. I felt anxious, but primarily excited to meet the first clients and discover my role with them. I stood up, walked around the room to work off some of my nervous energy, and to take in the sights and sounds of the room; he didn't seem to mind. I could still hear the click of my heels on the tile floor and still feel the heat of his breath on the back of my neck before I turned around to face another devil in disguise, a monster, a man who ripped out women's souls and gladly watched them shrivel and disappear under his weight. His only concern was power. I take that back. He had two concerns: power and pain—those were his pleasures.

His cold brown eyes burrowed down on me, and he placed his forehead against mine, hard. The force knocked me back slightly, but he pursued quickly, and he forced his lips against mine as if he were trying to burst the blood out of them like grapes. I tried to push him away, but he gained strength; my body froze again, paralyzed, and those dirty, dirty hands began to remove my clothes while I begged him to stop.

Wilderness

I plummeted to the lowest point in my life thus far, stuck in a wilderness, a holding pattern of marching around in circles and never getting anywhere. I heard a story once about Jean-Henri Fabre studying some processionary caterpillars who walked in circles for eight days—only inches from food, in a rut of paralysis, stuck without direction—until they fell over dead from starvation. My life was that of a processionary caterpillar. I was paralyzed by repetitive, self-destructive behavior.

As I mentioned previously, I experimented sexually after adolescence. Prior to sixteen, prior to my very, very late puberty—I didn't start puberty until I reached sixteen—my sexual encounters were forced, dirty, and abusive. At nearly seventeen, I decided to have consensual sex for the first time. I chose whose hands touched me this time—this time I was in control.

A week or so before I turned seventeen, Momma lay on the couch curled ever so slightly with her head resting in the notch between the armrest and the back of the couch. Her diaphragm and ribs raised and lowered slightly while she rested. I sneaked into the room.

"Momma?"

No answer.

"Momma?"

Silence. Exhale, inhale, exhale, inhale, a slight twist of her body, one toe pressing into the heel of her other foot. She pushed her sock down a bit. Silence.

"Momma, I am going to do it. I am going to have sex. This is my choice. I've planned it out. We'll be safe, but I think it's time."

Silence. Surely Momma played possum too. I guess the apple didn't fall too far from the tree. For the next two days, I got the same response from Momma that I got when I tried to talk to her about sex. Silence. Then, she called up my boyfriend, and she invited him over. She had "the talk" with him, the one she never had with me. Later, she took me to the doctor for a physical and we got contraceptives. She never discussed saving myself for marriage, my body being sacred and special—not a playground on which boys find titillation—or discovering true love.

In my family, among the women, we understood what it meant to be second. Actually, being second had its advantages. Today, a pejorative term exists for this position, a second lover is called a "side ho." That term is demeaning and harmful, yet it creates a boundary—on the side. The lady on the side didn't have to deal with all the drama of a real relationship. She could get what she wanted or needed: attention, sex, money, a date, power, control, authority, desire, and then move on. Momma wasn't worried about me saving myself or finding love; she wanted to make sure I wielded my power correctly.

But I didn't. My boyfriend and I arrived at a nasty "roach motel," the kind where the patrons pay by the hour, and we had sex. The experience caused no physical pain, but it was incredibly anticlimactic and emotionally scarring. I remember lying in between the covers on my side, watching his bare back and backside disappear into the restroom after we finished, and feeling the remaining pieces of my heart slide despairingly into my stomach. I wondered if that was it, and then curled up like a pill bug. The loss of my virginity created one of the most deflating and gut-wrenching experiences of my life—the experience of feeling deep regret over giving my body away so cheaply. I was meaningless. I had given myself, my whole body, to this boy, and for nothing. As with all addictions, I did not know at the time what I had bit into; I only knew now, though I hated it, I felt empty without it.

Just like the processionary caterpillar, I fell into a pattern. Sex never fulfilled, it was not enjoyable, nor rewarding, but I could garner control and I could garner attention, so I began to give my body away freely. This same story repeats itself, over and over, off the lips of many different women. They have sex the first time, and it is lack-luster, disruptive, and disturbing. Rather than learning from the experience, the all-or-nothing mentality takes over and all seems lost. They gave themselves away once, so why stop? Now, all that is left to do is "it." And they do. Multiple times with multiple men or women, and they find themselves stuck in a rut, seeking love that can't be fully satisfied through sex. So they continue, as I did, like the processionary caterpillar, killing themselves.

I continued marching in this sexual cycle throughout high school and right into college, searching for meaning in something that was supposed to be meaningful, but using it in a meaningless way. You know, chemotherapy can be very meaningful for the cancer patient—a last lifeline—but for one who doesn't have cancer, chemotherapy applied in a meaningless way would only lead to death. Sex delivered the same outcome, but instead of death, I'll use a synonym for death to describe it—lifeless.

I continued this lifestyle in school, but I had no direction, and sexual experiences took their toll on my young heart and body. I found myself lying lifeless, detached, paralyzed, and in a parched wilderness.

Paralyzed

And that is exactly how I found myself at Splash. Forced on my back, my skirt hiked up, my shirt ripped open, and begging the man, "Please don't do this! Please don't do this!" Let me be clear: I did not consent. I tried to fight. I resisted. I pushed him away, I struggled with his hands, but he just kept coming after me. He penetrated. And I gave in.

I started to cry, meaningless, meaningless tears. The tears never stopped anyone in the past. Everybody just did with my body what they wished; the tears, sobs, and screams never stopped anyone. They actually seemed to encourage them. But right now, I could feel his body undulating back and forth, back and forth, but I detached. I shut my heart and mind off, but the meaningless tears kept flowing.

Thrust after ferocious thrust, he grew more aggressive. He clung to me, squeezing with his fingers wrapped around my arms, little pieces of dirt underneath his white fingernails. I squeezed back; I squeezed and clenched and let my body fight the battle while my mind detached. I think he was angry, trying to punish me, trying to punish women for what they had done to him. He grunted and groaned, but I kept my silence. He didn't stop when I had begged and cried, so I didn't give him the satisfaction of thinking he could hurt me. I cried for me, not because of him, but for me. He increased his tempo. I counted the fish. On the walls several fish were painted all around the room, and as he pleasured himself at my expense, I counted the fish, and the rocks in the tanks, and the swimming fish. People passed by in the hallways; I could hear mind-numbing chitter chatter as they walked up and down the halls, unknowing of the atrocity taking place inside the next room. I counted the rocks, tiny droplets of red and green iridescent pebbles in the bottom of the fish tanks. I flatlined. I could hear his breathing—stinky, sweaty, panting. I could hear the discordant sounds of guitars and screams of Kurt Cobain wailing, "Rape me, rape me my friend! / Rape me, rape me again!"—and then I heard silence.

For a moment, all I heard was silence—deafening silence. And for a moment more, I heard nothing. I thought, *Am I deaf?* Until I heard a familiar sound, a familiar voice, "Stupid, stupid, stupid. You're so stupid! Stupid. How could you let this happen? Stupid. You're so stupid, stupid, stupid . . ." My voice. How could I be so stupid?

I wonder. I wonder if he thought the same thing about himself when he stopped. I wonder if he struggled for manhood, for power, for control, for love, for acceptance, while he raped me. I wonder if the fact that I just lay there crying and counting silently, but never wincing, infuriated him, made him feel less of a man. I wonder if when he finished, as his body returned to normal and his brain downshifted, did he tell himself the same thing? *I'm stupid. So stupid. Why do I keep doing this? Stupid.*

Weight

I have never told this story before—except to Momma—and doing so brings up tremendous emotions. An incredible weight comes with sexual abuse, and especially rape; it ties you down to a specific moment you only wish to escape. Telling my story lifts the weight somewhat, but it's also a bitter reminder of the weight, especially the weight I felt when I stood up.

When I stood up after being raped, I felt dizzy. Something . . . different, but not quite sure what. I barely heard anything, other than my own recurrent self-deprecations, *Stupid, stupid*, and I stumbled, hardly walking. I got fully dressed, and we left Splash. We never met any clients there. I guess I was it.

Afterwards, we drove to a local fast-food, greasy-burger joint, and he treated me to lunch. I write that with the utmost sarcasm intended, although in the moment, I followed him around submissively, blessed to be in his presence. My emotions anchored back to my first abuse as a child, paralyzed in time, so I did as I was told. I finished the work he had for that day, he paid me, and then I caught the bus home. Only I didn't go home. I went to my Momma's house.

Clearly, I appeared rattled and empty, but nobody asked me what happened. I suppose they thought that Shree was in one of her funky moods. I didn't have the words to tell them what had happened; I didn't want to. I stayed for a while, and then I went home, a gnawing ache inside me. I wanted to tell someone so badly, but the weight wouldn't let me. I felt so stupid, so dirty and stupid.

In the shower at home, I cried and cried, but nothing cleansed me. The tears couldn't get the feeling out, and the water couldn't wash away the stains. I let the steam form all around me, the hot water ran until it was cold and I shivered and shook, teeth chattering while goosebumps rose and faded, but I was stuck—weighted down—and I couldn't feel clean. The crying and showering did nothing but saturate me, pull me down, drown me, so I cried myself to sleep, wrapped in a cold, wet towel upon my bed, knowing I could never tell. I had bragged about this job, the company car, the future, so I'd never tell anybody. I was paralyzed by shame.

The weight only increased. My face disfigured when I smiled, which was less and less often each day. Depression sneaked in and enveloped me like a cloak and pinned itself up tightly, wrapping around and around and around until I couldn't move from the sheer weight of it. My face dragged. I had Bell's palsy—my face was literally paralyzed—depression, and self-loathing. I stopped showering and doing self-care. My weight dropped from 125 pounds to 110 pounds, but I still felt heavier. Nothing mattered. I moved back in with Momma.

Although I quit showering, quit brushing my hair, quit caring, somehow, I worked up enough energy to get out of bed and find a job at a mail-packing store. The elderly gentleman who ran the place opened new possibilities. His warm energy helped me trust again, slightly. His hands were genuine and his heart seemed full of compassion. He taught me how to balance a checkbook, how to treat customers, how to run a business. He slowly instilled bits and pieces of wisdom, ever-so-patiently, and propped me back on my feet. We continued in these long conversations that usually ended with his walking away and my thinking about a story he had just told. He told stories and politely left me to figure them out. During the middle of one of his stories, I looked him in his pale, blue eyes, standing across the counter as he packed a box with contents and packaging peanuts. His words lost meaning, their message incomprehensible. His face swelled, and then blurred, and then I saw nothing.

His eyes staring into mine were the first things I saw when I woke up lying on the mailroom floor. A few days later, Momma took me to see the doctor. Waiting in his office, I felt the weight in the pit of my stomach. Something wasn't right, my face drooped, my brain fogged, I couldn't move. Then the doctor told me I had a terminal illness. Life as I knew it was over—I was pregnant.

I realize now my thinking was entirely melodramatic. Pregnancy should be a time of celebration, but I was young, and the weight I then carried had an emotional handicap attached to it. While we slumped down the corridor to leave the doctor's office, I told Momma I was pregnant. To her, it was nearly insignificant, pregnancy was a part of life. As we neared the exit, I could feel my left hand beginning to scrape the wall, right across my knuckles, then my left shoulder, then my head, rubbing against the wall. I slid down the wall and collapsed in a basket of confusion.

I didn't know why I was pregnant. I didn't know if it was my boyfriend's baby or if it was from the rape. I didn't know how to escape. Shrouded in confusion and lumped in a pile against the wall in the doctor's office foyer, I did know some things. I didn't want to have a baby. Having a baby was expensive. Having a baby was a burden. I didn't want to be on welfare. I didn't want to be . . .

During my high school experience, I said repeatedly I would never have an abortion. I was that girl. I knew abortion killed, and I would never do that to my child. But now that I was actually faced with the decision, I knew I couldn't carry what lived inside me. I write *what* because I felt detached. Paralyzed by pain, stuck in the wilderness, carrying this weight too big for me to carry, I decided to have the abortion.

I don't want to write about the clinic. Every time I think about it, I only remember tears and blood and fluid and death. I feel the cold, sterile room, the latex gloves, the tugging both at my heart and my body, and the sense something irreversible has been done. Later in my life, I thanked my parents for not having an abortion with me—I was unexpected, unplanned, too early. My child will never get the chance to thank me.

Shame crept in—shame with a face that looked like mine but with hollow eyes, a lopsided smile, and no heart. Shame crept in and carried me away. I did something I said I would never do. I became someone I thought I would never become. I wrestled with myself and my thoughts, looking for a way out of who I was. There was no way out of the wilderness; I must have been born for this.

Resilient

Core

"We need women [and men] who are so strong they can be gentle, so educated they can be humble, so fierce they can be compassionate, so passionate they can be rational, and so disciplined they can be free."–Kavita Ramdas

By now, the words I have used to describe my life and my upbringing—*shattered, paralyzed, scarred, abused, molested, raped, dead*—may have worn thin and made you wonder if I am reveling in my pain and basking in the glory of telling the story of my injuries. If I am, then I am stuck, and you have no reason to read my story unless you desire another night of heartache, so you can at least feel something. No, my intent is not to manifest all of my hurts and woes to the world; my hope is to set a foundation to build upon. In order to begin to see the *trust* in the **strug**gles, the *silence* in **resiliency**, the *rest* in shat**te**red, the *zeal* in **par**alyzed, the *use* in ab**used**, one must begin to look at life and its circumstances hopefully. If not, he or she will only see *hatred* in sh**att**ered, *raped* in **par**alyzed, *less* in strug**gles**, and *lies* in **resil**iency. We don't wallow in our past, but we look at the past to allow us to learn for the present.

One of the lessons we must learn together is that our brokenness does not define who we are. If others have treated us haphazardly or with contempt, we cannot be defined by it: we must continue to grow and learn—through the adversity. However, if we, in our brokenness and selfishness, go around hurting others, then, yes, we must change. We must find the zeal within us and direct it for the good of others.

After my rape and abortion, I moved a few times until I finally moved in with Kim and Pam. During that time, while I attended junior college and lived with them, I began working on developing a set of beliefs that would get me through life. The way Kim and Pam loved me without expecting anything in return helped set the precedent for these beliefs. My relationship with God solidified the beliefs, and slowly, with trial, error, and a very intentional work toward healing, I began escaping my past. These beliefs helped me through my education, my career, my relationships, and my healing. Practicing these beliefs helped me heal and helped me lead others to healing. Healing must be at the core.

Hurdles

I used to run the hurdles. In high school and college, I ran track, and in college I ran the 400m hurdles and the 100m hurdles, but the 400m was my favorite. However, the 100m hurdles would make me dig down into the core of who I was, explode out of the blocks, power over the hurdles, land in motion, dig deep through the screaming muscles, and sprint it out at the end. Running the 100m hurdles is not only about leaving your all on the track, all the way down the core, and sprinting your heart out; it is also about cadence and rhythm. You have to watch your steps. For me, since I would switch jumping legs over each hurdle, my steps were ordered: seven from the block and three between each hurdle. In the mind of a hurdler, it would sound something like this: *Set. Bang! One, two, three, four, five, six, seven, HIT! One, two, three, HIT! One, two, three, HIT! One, two, three, HIT! One, two, three, HIT! One, two, three, HIT!* And so on until you cleared the last hurdle and sprinted out the finish, exhilarated and exhausted at the same time.

Let me paint the picture for you; this may deepen your understanding if you imagine yourself running the hurdles. As you walk to the starting line across the smoldering track that is black as tar, with heat rising through the aggregate rubber, your heart begins to lurch up toward your throat. The sensation in your calf muscles is one of tension; you're walking on your heels to keep your spikes up off the track. Drops of sweat trickle from your brow to your cheek and absorb into your uniform, some roll down your rib cage, while others fly listlessly from your legs in motion. Your pulse elevates. You can feel it in your chest, your eyes, your temples. The crowd noise blurs into indistinct sounds as a blessed breeze blows softly past your ears. You close your eyes, inhale deeply, and allow your lungs to fill with oxygen. You close your eyes and search for peace. The starting official calls you to your blocks. Down you crouch, one leg curled back, foot pressed against the block, which you compress down like a coiled spring. You shake the other leg, sweat falls, you remember to breathe. Now you back down the other leg, the rear leg, set deeper in the blocks. Your foot locks against the block and you place your hands at the starting line, measured out two hand lengths—forefinger to thumb—from your center, and you keep your hands in the same position while you rest back for one brief moment. Head down. The sweat drips one final, translucent drip and splashes against the track. Rock forward. Your heart stops. Your breathing stops. Sound stops and a rumbling fills your ears. You raise your eyes, not your head, and you can hear again. "Set!" calls the starter. Chin up, your breathing stops again, your triceps shudder, butt up, back slightly arched, then *bang!* Sound and wind fill your ears, your heart now races out of your chest, arms pumping dramatically, feet flying, leaning forward, but pushing to get to a nearly upright state, seventh step. *HIT!*

One thing that never surprised me was the hurdles. I never walked to the track and said, "What!? There are hurdles here today! How am I supposed to run? What do I do now? Please, Lord, please deliver me from these ten plagues placed before me! You promised to make my paths straight, and now there are these hurdles!" I never once turned to my friends and said, "Can you believe this? There are hurdles on the track. This is ridiculous. What are we supposed to do?" I never folded my arms, sat down, crossed my legs, and pouted. When I walked up to the track, I wasn't shocked by the hurdles; I expected them.

And this leads me to my ten core beliefs—ten beliefs that help me overcome the hurdles of life. And there will be hurdles. Don't be surprised.

10 Core Beliefs

When I was almost finished with high school, I began having dreams about trees, trees only found in a temperate deciduous forest, trees we didn't have in L.A. The dreams descended, poignant but irrelevant, yet I believed that someday I would know the meaning behind those dreams.

As a child, I was told many times that my "head was in the clouds" or that "I dreamed too much," and I thought something was wrong with me, but I did not stop dreaming. When I decided to go to school to become a teacher, I believed it was possible for me to be a teacher, in spite of my upbringing. Regardless of growing up in a single-parent home, the child of a negligent father, a victim of abuse, one from south of Central Avenue in L.A., and, maybe most notably, a black female to boot, I continued to believe my dreams could become reality. What kept me going was my belief that all things were possible, and winners are not determined by how they start, but how they finish. Sure, I encountered detours, many of which I have confided in you, some I haven't, but the detours didn't determine the final destination. The belief did.

Core Belief #1: I Believe in the Possibilities.

I haven't arrived. I know that, so I don't know what my final destination in this life will be, but I do know believing in the possibilities has led me to many significant arrivals. I believed in these possibilities from a young age. Thus, pretending to be a teacher as a child, writing curriculum, studying with friends, doing work by candlelight, studying philosophy and literature—even though I didn't do well in high school—were activities I chose to do because I believed in the possibility I could become a teacher. The belief led to action, and the actions multiplied across time morphed the belief into a reality.

As my plane descended over Nashville, when I moved from L.A. to attend Fisk University, I saw the trees of my dreams. Teems of them. I saw the dreaming trees out of the window and knew my childhood dreams were becoming a reality. The goal at that time was to finish school and teach. Now, multiple degrees later, teaching on the secondary, the university, and the career/business levels, I realize my first core belief turned a possibility into a reality. How I started didn't matter; what matters is how I run the race and how I finish.

To overcome the hurdle of disbelief, look for the possibilities and take the next step. For me, it was to take the steps to become a teacher. What is it for you?

Inspiration

No Name also came from a single-parent home in South Central L.A., under extreme poverty, and ended up attending a famed Texas university. The made-for-TV movie, which I can't list here since he has no name, chronicles his upbringing, but avoids much of the true depravity surrounding his young life. No Name was an incredible student, hard-working and academically versatile; he didn't just go to school on his football skills (although he did run a 4.24 in the 40-yard dash), he went to school on his smarts, resiliency, work ethic, and kindness to others. In spite of the failings in our relationship, No Name inspires me. He inspires me due to where he came from and where he is going. Today, No Name still gives back by working with underprivileged children and students in the community, even by working with those who were in the juvenile correction facilities in the past. No Name was and is one in ten million.

Core Belief #2: I Am Inspired by Others

If you'll notice, my core beliefs are written as "I" statements. Now, this isn't meant to exclude you; this is designed to inspire you and to help you write your own. If my core beliefs help you overcome life's hurdles, use them. If you have some unique core beliefs of your own, then write them down. I wrote mine due to the inspiration of others.

I am inspired by others, and especially by their stories—both triumphant and despairing. When I need encouragement, or when I need to believe people can do good, I look to the stories of others. Kendrick Lamar came from the streets of Compton to go on to win a Pulitzer Prize for music. T. D. Jakes came from a shack in West Virginia, where he cared for his invalid father. At the time, he pastored a church of nearly ten members. Now, he pastors a church in Dallas, TX, with approximately twenty thousand members—one of the largest churches in America. God spoke the world into existence, including the sky, grass, trees, and fruit. Steve Jobs took ideas about passing language and thoughts across space and time and gave us Apple. Now, you speak into a device, and it does what you want it to do; sometimes it creates what you want it to create. Serena Williams broke the mold for tennis like Jackie Robinson did for baseball. Malcolm X, the butterfly of the civil rights movement, underwent a great awakening and helped change American history forever. Don't judge Malcolm X on his worst times—nobody wants to be judged on who he or she was, especially for something he or she did in the dark—look at who Malcolm X became in the end. Although at one time he rejected the civil rights movement, taught black supremacy, and disavowed racial integration, in the end he began working with the civil rights movement, detested racism, and sought unity of all races. Stories of changing, overcoming obstacles, and progressing through life to arrive at a more-enriched state inspire me.

Since I know I am inspired by the stories of others, I seek them out. I read biographies and memoirs, watch speeches, listen to podcasts, and, most importantly, I talk to people. I look for the story from the lady at the supermarket who has become sober, attended rehab, relapsed, attended rehab again, and now is finishing school. Or the man who lost his leg in a motorcycle accident and is now using his story to inspire both amputees and non-amputees alike. I look for inspiration from others. To overcome the hurdle of circumstantial woe, look to others for inspiration.

Convincing Arguments

In the Jewish culture, the pupils often walked in the shadow of and worked alongside the Jewish rabbis. Education, was not simply a "sit and get" type of experience, but rather a dynamic relationship of giving and taking, with the rabbi holding the prominent seat and wielding great authority. The closer one walked to the rabbi, the more he could learn.

Jesus was a considerable rabbi, historically, the most influential. On one occasion he taught His disciples, "If you abide in my word, you are truly my disciples, and you will know the truth, and the truth will set you free" (John 8:31–32).

Maintaining belief in the possibilities and searching to be inspired by others takes work. I have to live in it. I have to study the possibilities, which means I have to be intentional about looking for the possibilities. I have to look for the inspirational stories, seek them out, digest them, and I have to believe they are true and possible. Sure, I can take the easy route and be cynical, but cynicism is not living in the truth;

cynicism is confining myself to the constraints of my own thinking and experience. It disregards the truth. I have to convince myself of the truth.

Core Belief #3: I Convince Myself of the Truth

Yes, I unashamedly read the Bible and believe it to be true. I also seek out Papa through prayer and ask Him to reveal the truth to me. Then I set about convincing myself of its truth. When I was young, fresh into college at Los Angeles Southwest College, still suffering depression from my rape and the abortion I had, truth looked awfully bleak. I looked destined for failure, sexual promiscuity, depravity, and a self-seeking lifestyle. Living that way would have been easier; I could have remained cynical.

I chose to convince myself of the truth. So I cracked open my Bible, cracked open my journal, cracked open my mind, my ears, and my heart, and I started writing. I made lists: I am fearfully and wonderfully made; I am forgiven; I am a conqueror; I am God's daughter; I am the perfect weight; I am beautiful; I am comfortable in my own skin; I hear God's voice; I follow God's voice; my intentions are pure; I have faith; I have joy; I reflect soulful beauty; I am organized; I am a lender, not a borrower; my steps are ordered—think back to the hurdles—; and I am free in spirit! I did not believe what I was writing to be true; rather, I had to *convince* myself of the truth.

This idea of writing out or speaking the truth to convince yourself is not new. Read the psalms. David did it over and over and over. If the Bible or religion is not inspirational to you, look to other people. Remember Muhammad Ali? "I am the greatest! I am the king of the world!" Surely, he didn't believe all those superlatives originally. He had to convince himself, in that time and space, he was the greatest—and he was. In the personal development arena, self-talk cards are often cited as being responsible for the most dramatic changes in personal behavior and self-esteem. Sometimes, you have to sell the truth to yourself.

So it was a choice. I could remain locked in cynicism, a prisoner in the cell of circumstance, crying out against the world and the fell clutch it had on me, or I could choose to live, to work, and to abide. Disregarding my failures, shedding the skin of my colorful past, daily, I worked to convince myself of the truth. Often, I failed; often, I succeeded. I journaled, made lists, repeated phrases and words both audibly and inaudibly, and I convinced myself. I made a choice.

Be convinced your life is meaningful, and you can be free.

Freedom Marches

I love to walk the trails around Nashville, the woods and greenery before me as they pass by on my right, left, and overhead, listening to the sounds of the chirping birds intermingled with the crunching dirt beneath my feet, and looking at the squirrels playing in the grass while the smells of trees and grass and flowers fill me up. Along these trails I often meet characters, different characters: mothers on walks with their children, exercise enthusiasts in tight workout apparel cycling or running past, teenagers trying to escape the demands of their parents if only for but a moment, students, nomads, the homeless.

One day, I met a man with flowing, silver hair that narrowed to an unkempt white beard and covered a vivacious smile. His eyes were blue and his feet were bare; he wore a tie-dye t-shirt and a hemp necklace. He greeted me with a smile, and although I had some reticent fears, I struck up a conversation out of respect. He looked so free, so one with himself and nature, and the marijuana smell wafting my way let me know he thought he was free from the law in Tennessee at that time. Maybe he was on a freedom march like I was, feeling free and enjoying who I was, where I was, with the company I met.

His smile quickly faded. As we talked, I could hear the resentment and the weary pain from his past. He had worked in law previously, and his body language demonstrated an uncomfortable feeling, bitterness eking out of his pores. We lost eye contact, his movements became erratic, and his speech showed he wasn't happy with the city, with the state, with people, with life in general. He was a façade—a mirage of freedom like an African herd of antelope running swiftly through the savannah unaware of the high fences holding them captive for the evening hunts. He appeared free, but he was a prisoner in his own skin, undisciplined in his rhetoric—as evidenced by his constant complaining—and defined by cynicism. He needed acceptance; I hope he found it.

Core Belief #4: I Am Free in Spirit

A person who is free in spirit is positively infectious, disciplined in who she is, and comfortable in her own skin. Freedom is a result of discipline. Nations didn't become free without discipline, and those who have lost their freedom—individuals, not nations or people groups who have been enslaved—lost it due to a lack of discipline. In order to have a positively infectious personality and be comfortable in one's own skin, one has to be—I have to be—disciplined.

My personal discipline is to stay connected with a Higher Being and to myself. For me, I have to engage Papa in a relationship, through discourse, reading, listening, and obeying. I have to discipline myself to make decisions supporting His desires and what He has said about me. Those lists I made, the ones I use to convince myself of the truth, I had to discipline myself to make those lists, and then discipline myself to ask, "Does the decision I am about to make bring me closer to the truth or take me further away?" I disciplined myself to greet people, to think of others first, to treat people with respect, and to believe the truth.

Invoking discipline allows me to become comfortable in my own skin. One evening I was sitting at dinner at a very large gathering for a very prestigious business. We were seated at tables, surrounded by people we didn't know, and everyone and everything exuded elegance. The table brimmed with platters and plates, cups, silverware, napkins, and decorations galore. Eating wasn't the primary objective, behaving in a civilized, high-society fashion was. I didn't even know which fork to use. Everyone at the table sat prim and proper, making small talk and giving awkward glances. Were we supposed to eat? I didn't know, but I was hungry. I looked at the lady next to me and said, "Ma'am, which fork are we supposed to use?"

She said, "I don't know. I thought you knew. I was waiting for you!"

We both laughed with our eyes and our mouths, and then I picked up a fork and began to dig in. So did the rest of the table. If I had not disciplined myself to be the initiator of conversation, the first to ask questions, the seeker of answers to help and support others, we would probably all still be sitting at that table today looking very, very skinny. To be free in spirit is to be comfortable with who you are, and you become comfortable with who you are by discipling yourself.

Once you know who you are by convincing yourself of the truth, being inspired by others, and believing in the possibilities for yourself, you can become positively infectious. A happy person, a person who is generous with himself, his time, his smile, his laughter, but who is disciplined enough not to lose himself to the desires of his body or a desperate need for attention, is positively infectious. He is able to dance with his daughters, sing to his wife, build with his brothers, and cry with his mother. He doesn't avoid; he engages. But this man, or woman, does not happen by accident. He is a result of disciplined action leading to a defined result—freedom in spirit.

A good way to start determining who you are is to look to a Higher Being. Take a walk, ask questions, listen, make it a freedom march so you can seek out freedom in spirit. I am unashamedly a Christ-follower. I have friends of all different religions, ethnicities, ages, sexual orientations, occupations, and I love all of them—while holding true to who I am and what I believe. I have meaningful engagements with people of different opinions and values and still remain who I am. I am *poor* in spirit, and out of that poverty comes my freedom, since I have nothing holding me down. Therefore, I can let go because I have nothing to lose and everything to gain. Poor people know they are poor; they don't have to be convinced something better is out there and they have little to lose. My poverty in spirit provokes me to reach for Christ; He tells me the truth, and He sets me free.

Conquests

At the beginning of my story, I told you about a time when everything was a battle. Just getting up in the morning was a battle. We didn't have electricity—except from the generator—the home was roach-infested, bodies were all over, and the key ingredient holding everyone together was sleep, except for me. I got up, got ready, and walked the long walk to school. Each day was a reminder that obstacles were a guarantee and I had very little control. Life taught me that; I couldn't even control what happened to my body. So my choices were either to walk on or curl up.

Core Belief #5: I Am a Conqueror

Viktor Frankl said, "When we are no longer able to change a situation, we are challenged to change ourselves." One of my core beliefs is I am a conqueror; I will overcome. I am responsible for my attitude and my approach to obstacles. Earlier, I introduced you to the four monsters: the fear monster, the trust monster (doubt), the inadequacy monster (perfectionism), and the unworthy monster (loneliness). My childhood reinforced that these monsters existed, and that they owned me—I could not escape. My skin color, the shape of my body, my failures, and even my occupation served as a reminder of these monsters, the ones with friendly faces who tell me lies—*I have to protect myself;*

overcomers rely on themselves, not others; I like to do things the right way; I have to do it by myself to prove I am strong enough to do it.

I am not surprised by the obstacles, the lies, the monsters; I expect them, and I have a plan for them. The plan sounds something like: *One, two, three, HIT! One, two, three, HIT! One, two, three, HIT!* When a lie attacks me or I face an obstacle, I fight back. A false belief, I combat with a convincing truth. A bad report—maybe in my work or from the doctor—I look for an opportunity to improve or a battle strategy. Of all of my core beliefs, this is probably the least profound, but one of the most important. Anticipating conflict does not mean predicting negative future events, it means predetermining that you will do whatever it takes to conquer. Life is a battle, it's a race; you have to have a strategy. When I was in school it looked something like this: Plan A: graduate college; Plan B: enforce Plan A.

Everyone

In the rear of the classroom at Jere Baxter Alternative School sat a young Hispanic boy we'll call Rico. He had his head down, his hoodie up, and his earbuds in. In my classroom, everyone knew we did not wear hats or hoods, we did not have phones out or earbuds in, and we did not, did not lay our heads down on the desk. Everything about Rico's posture exuded disrespect, from his sagging pants, to the fact that he even had a hoodie on, which was out of uniform. I walked to the back of the room, knelt down, and asked him if he was ill. He popped out one earbud.

"Leave me alone!" he growled.

Profanity was off-limits in my classroom.

"Okay, honey, I just thought maybe you were sick."

"I'm not."

I placed my hand on his shoulder, not knowing if it was going to further irritate him or bring him a sense of calm. His body trembled. He tensed up and his shoulders shook. I had to act quickly, get him out of there before anyone saw—he was crying.

I whispered, "Ignore what I say and come with me." I grabbed his hoodie with my clenched hand, twisted it, and in a raised voice said, "Rico, come with me, young man! You know you can't wear that hoodie in here or have those earbuds in. Come with me out in the hall now!" I whirled him around before the other students could see and marched him out in the hall, slamming the door behind me.

The other students began to chatter, "What's up with Ms. Walker, yo?" and "Walk must be real hot today!" I could hear them through the door confirming I had diverted their attention. I looked up at Rico, watched him wipe his face, and asked him what was wrong.

"My dad, Miss. My dad, he kicked my brother out the house yesterday. He keeps sayin' my brother's disrespectful, but he's the one who's disrespectful. Always drunk. Never keepin' a job for more than a month or two. My brother's my best friend, Miss. He's the only one who keeps me sane."

I knew this wasn't typical. This wasn't Rico's typical behavior, and honestly, without stereotyping too much, this wasn't my typical experience with my Hispanic students. Most Latino families I knew had both parents in the home, and their fathers worked hard. I knew Rico must have felt like an outcast, even among his people. Now, he had lost his brother.

Rico took off his hoodie and went to the restroom to clean up. When he returned to class, I let him sit in the back of the room. The next day, I spoke with him before class and after class. I kept up with his family. I made sure in our class he was always at the center of the activity, always a leader, always given a choice to be heard. He deserved both. He deserved to be allowed to show his pain and to be heard. I made sure of it. One thing Rico wanted, one thing all teenage boys want, one thing everyone wants, is to be treated with respect.

Core Belief #6: I Deserve to Treat Everyone with Respect.

Engagement is key, and it is a core responsibility of a person desiring respect. Because I desire respect from others, I deserve to respect others and to engage others. If they disengage, for whatever reason, that is their choice. My responsibility is to engage, and I do this by speaking first, offering a hand to shake or help, and by letting them know I see them. Whether it is a student with his head down in class, a homeless man, a black business woman in a traditionally white work place, or a white woman in a traditionally black hair salon, I deserve to treat everyone with respect.

I see color. I embrace color. Some people say they don't see color, but all that does is make me . . . invisible. That's exactly what we want to erase. Color can be part of culture, but it doesn't define a person. One black person may be from the trailer park, the other from Compton, the other from an Ivy League school, and the other from Nigeria. Their commonality is their skin tone, but their experiences are diverse.

I want people to see each other's color, to celebrate their color, to keep them visible, to show respect. I don't want you or me to assign experience by color. That's disrespectful to the other person and to our own vision. It limits me, and it limits you.

Now, don't be fooled. I fail in this area too. Being black doesn't mean that I don't judge, and being a black female from L.A. who now teaches on the university level doesn't mean I always treat people with respect. I fail. This is a core *belief*, not a walk of perfection. After I fail, I make amends, and I get up and do the right thing—again.

I deserve to treat people with respect because I am one decision away from being that person. I am one decision away from being a doctor, and one decision away from being homeless. I am one decision away from using my hands to write a best seller, or using them to insert a drug needle. I am one move from bumping into a famous movie producer, and one move from falling and having a traumatic brain injury. I am one word away from being disrespectful.

I deserve to treat people with respect because anyone can be redeemed. The Bible overflows with stories of men and women who were scandalous yet sought and received redemption. I deserve to treat people with respect because we all have scars, and our scars are what make us beautiful; they represent what we have overcome. I deserve to treat everyone with respect because the man with scars on His hands, feet, and side was once on death row, and "[His] grace is sufficient for you" and me.

Great Expectations

The lights flashed once, twice; the clock stood at 12:05 and the bell rang to begin class. I closed the door. Exactly two minutes and fifteen seconds later, a student we'll call Mercutio came bursting through the door. He was late, and he was deaf. He hadn't heard the bell. In that classroom at Hillsboro High School, the students, all of them with IEPs, had created a list of rules and consequences. One rule was to be present in class, on time, prepared, and in your seat. The consequence was to stand in the corner. Their rule. Their consequence.

When I told Mercutio he had to go stand in the corner, the rest of the students grew upset. They thought it unjust to have a deaf student suffer the consequences of not hearing a bell. I stood my ground. I explained the bell rang the same time every day. We had clocks in the hallways, signs on the walls, the flow of student traffic in and out of the classrooms, lights flashed before the bell sounded, and we also had all the other days when Mercutio had been punctual to demonstrate he knew when and how to get to class on time. I did all this explaining *after* I had asked Mercutio why he was late. Everyone didn't agree, but Mercutio had to stand in the corner. Maybe it seems rough, but the reason those students were able to pass the end-of-year assessment despite their disabilities was they worked hard, and I had high expectations both for them and for me.

Core Belief #7: I Have High Expectations for Myself and Others

During weddings, the minister will stand before the crowd and read from 1 Corinthians 13, "the love chapter," to encourage the couple to love each other patiently, kindly, with humility, and everlastingly. He or she will admonish the couple that love "does not envy or boast; it is not arrogant or rude . . . it does not rejoice at wrongdoing, but rejoices with the truth." The minister will quote how love "bears all things, believes all things, hopes all things, endures all things" and that love "never ends." Rarely does the minister expound on "believes all things."

Having high expectations for myself and others does not mean having unreasonable expectations, and then condemning myself or others when we fail. Because we will. What it means is to *believe* even if someone has failed in the past, and we *hope* he or she will do the right thing this time, even though the individual has a history of doing the wrong thing. We *bear* with the temper tantrums and lies in order to get to the core issue. To have high expectations for myself and for others is to love myself and others—to hope the best, and when we fall, to get up so we don't fail.

Engaged

She giggled next to me, squirmed in her, seat and laughed out loud. I had to scoot over, and I laughed too. Fifty-seven years old, having her first pedicure done, didn't know what to do, and she was completely ticklish. She engaged with life, and we had a wonderful time together getting our nails done. Before that day, I had never met her in my life. We had both sat in the salon separately, but after I engaged her in conversation, we laughed there together. She told me this was the first time she had a pedicure done. I walked her through the process, told her what to expect—except the ticklish part—and enjoyed her first pedicure with her. We had a meaningful experience, a meaningful engagement.

Core Belief #8: I Have Meaningful Engagements with Myself and Others

We are in this together! I have used the word *I* so many times throughout this memoir I have made myself sick. I am using my story and my experiences so you can see your story and your experiences in them, take what you need, and leave the rest. This interaction, between writer and reader, is a meaningful engagement. We can meet across time and space, at the meeting of the minds, and swap ideas. I anticipate your reading this; maybe you imagine my writing this, but we are both engaged, and it's meaningful.

The meeting in the nail salon was not orchestrated, it happened due to proximity. What made it meaningful was the shared experience—one we only shared because we engaged each other. Sometimes my days are just that, filled with quick moments with meaningful, heartfelt exchanges. Other times, I have deliberately set plans in order to engage friends or family. Remember the discipline? I have to schedule in meaningful engagements, even down to preparing conversation for when I get there. I don't mind small talk, but I want our relationship to have meaning, so I prepare for it.

A meaningful engagement with myself may mean a checkup from the neck up first thing in the morning. Maybe a poem and a cup of coffee around noon. A walk in the park. Time spent in front of my vision board, dreaming. A meaningful engagement with myself is when I take the time to get my mind right, so I can get my relationships right with others. I schedule those meetings too.

I have meaningful engagements with Papa all day long, one ongoing discourse. Petitions are made, prayers are answered, praise is offered. My engagements with Papa are not routine; they vary based on the discussion. At times, I get an answer right away, other times I have to wait, sometimes I argue back. Relationships provide direction in the darkness, a reason to persist through the wilderness, a will to live when all seems lost. They give meaning to life, so we must engage in them. Often.

Self

We have jumped eight hurdles and our legs are getting tired. We've hurdled over doubt by believing in the possibilities, we've jumped the comparison trap by allowing ourselves to be inspired by others, we've cleared the false lies by convincing ourselves of the truth, we've soared over obstacles by anticipating them and preparing ourselves to conquer them, we've flown over judgment by giving respect, we've graced over pride by disciplining ourselves to be free, we've launched over mediocrity with high expectations and love, we've bounded over apathy and lack of purpose by engaging meaningfully, and now we have come up against the most difficult hurdle of them all: number nine.

Hurdle number nine is an illusion. The hurdle appears as a mirror, but it reflects disingenuously. Hurdle nine transforms confidence into pride, humility into self-deprecation, hope into naivety, and purpose into stubbornness. Hurdle number nine is getting over yourself. You have to realize that you matter; if you don't you will spend all your time trying to make sure you matter. Unlike convincing yourself of the truth, to conquer hurdle number nine you must *accept* that you matter. You do have worth, you do have purpose, you are an inspiration to others.

Core Belief #9: I Am an Inspiration to Others (a Voice for the Voice-less).

Inspiration is a double-edged sword, it cuts both ways. Inspiration is coupled with influence, we can influence for both good and evil. We can influence someone to persist or to give up, but we have to realize we do have influence and we do inspire.

Because we are inspirational, we have responsibility. Stating, "I am an inspiration to others," is not some feeble attempt at self-actualiza-tion—it is a fact. As long as we come in contact with others, we will influence them. If we do something positive, eventually, this act will inspire others.

I have seen this fact as a teacher, a mentor, a friend, a principal, a student, a counselor, a sister, a daughter, a leader, a speaker, and a writer. Yes, I have a circle of influence. Yes, mine may be greater than some and smaller than others, but in order to hold myself accountable, I have to remember I matter and I inspire. So how do I do this? I take four steps:

1. I read inspiring literature, listen to inspiring music, and watch inspiring shows and movies.
2. I write inspirational messages to myself and others.
3. I speak inspiring words over myself and others.
4. I look for opportunities to inspire.

When it comes to hurdle number nine, we have to admit to ourselves that we influence others, which means we can inspire others. It doesn't matter how we feel—unless we are solitary on a deserted island—the statement "I am an inspiration to others" is a fact. But even on a deserted island we still impact the ecosystem. Maybe we inspire the fish.

I am an inspiration to others. I look for opportunities to inspire others. I exist for a purpose. I am an inspiration.

Born for This

At the end of the chapter "Paralysis," I finished with a statement, "I must have been born for this," in reference to my abuse. That statement is a lie. I was not born for brokenness; brokenness is a product of a broken world. You see, all of my core beliefs are all well and good until I measure them against death. I believe in the possibilities, until I die. I am inspired by others, until I die. I convince myself of the truth, until I am wrecked by the truth of the death of others or my own. I have high expectations, I am a conqueror, I am free in spirit, I have . . . all of these statements end when I die. They are temporal beliefs. So they'll get me through this life, but then what? Was I just born to die?

Core Belief #10: I Was Born to Be Redeemed.

To jump the final hurdle of death, we have to know our purpose. Inspiration is good, expectations are good, conquering is good, but they are not just limited to this world. If they were, then they would be meaningless because all would end in death. But death is not the end. My baby, the baby I never got to hold, has a purpose. He or she never got to live it out in this life, but he or she is living it out now in heaven. My purpose wasn't to be born here to be abused, raped, or mistreated. Neither was it to teach, inspire, live, and love here only. My true purpose has not yet been fully revealed.

I think of Hagar, walking in the desert, she and her son dying of thirst, but God preserved her for a greater purpose. I think of Jonah in the belly of a fish, preserved for a purpose. I think of myself hitting that tetherball, trying to get out all the pain, preserved for a purpose. We still read about Jonah and Hagar, millennia later, still carrying out their purpose, still influencing eternity.

We have a purpose here, no doubt. Our original purpose here was to live, to be fruitful, and multiply. But somebody messed that up. Somebodies. And a snake. But our eternal purpose hasn't been fully revealed yet. So for now I choose to follow Christ the best I know how, failing time and time again, with the full knowledge that in the end, I was born in blood and water, and in blood and water, I was redeemed.

Living

Writing out my ten core beliefs came easily, but the life I lived to learn them was hard. I feel like a hypocrite when I try to live them out daily. Although I know them and I have written them down, that doesn't mean I am good at them. I am still learning, and I am still learning to live them out.

I encourage you to determine your core beliefs, to write them out, and to commit to them. But I also encourage you to go on living. Get up when you think you have failed. The true failure is giving up. I write these words to myself as much as I do to you: when you fall down, get back up and keep going through it.

Walking Redemption

"Step out on faith and grow wings on the way down."–Shree Walker

A large, white schoolhouse stands in a painted meadow. With paned windows, rectangular in shape, and capped by semi-circle windows above, the school reflects the sun brilliantly across the meadow in which it sits, surrounded by children laughing, running, and playing, calling out to each other from under the blue sky and the willow trees. The grass rolls like waves under the breeze blowing from south to north, up and around the school, over the steps, and through the front door. In one window sits a red cardinal, singing his song, calling out, beckoning us to come and see his beauty and follow him inside. The school is a vivacious wheelhouse for learning, exploration, growing, teaching, and discovery. Everyone is welcome, and we all have something to teach and learn. This is how I imagine my life, my purpose here. My purpose is to be redeemed and to help others find their way to redemption. In the beginning, I didn't want to go to school, now, I imagine myself as a school—a safe place to learn, to teach, and to live.

Was it worth it? Was the walk to resiliency worth it? Did that young girl from the beginning of the story ever make it?

It was so worth it. This book is dedicated to the little girl inside: you are now free to heal. Walk on, little one, walk on.

Every day I learn something new as I unveil my scars and take out these broken pieces. I am not the same person I was five, four, three, two years ago. I am not the same person I was yesterday. The walk was so worth it. I am now free to heal.

My life came with scars, so I want to speak directly to those of you who have some scars. Revealing those scars, moving past those scars, embracing those scars is going to be difficult. You have the right to show you have been hurt, and you have the right to be heard. You also have the right to move past it. You can be free. You can feel. You can move past the monsters with friendly faces and acknowledge the scars.

Remember this, most people see the scars, but they don't see what is behind the scars. My scars have been masked by college degrees, a beautiful smile, a shapely body, an intellectual conversation, a gregarious attitude, nice clothes and cars, etc. But we both know what is behind the masks and scars. So the question is: What do we do about them? Let's use the scars, the pain, and learning that accompanied the scars to make us extraordinary. Who goes through all that just to be ordinary? Our pasts were extraordinary, so let's make our futures extraordinary. Let's choose to be great at any task we receive.

I still want to be a great teacher, but not just to students in the classroom. I want to be like the schoolhouse, a place of refuge for the students, the parents, the teachers, the community. I want to teach students at the university, the teenager who is down and out, the college-aged kid who can't balance a checkbook, the preacher who has nearly given up because his congregation has turned on him, the eternal pessimist I met on my walk, my neighbors, my friends, the lady at the nail salon, and my abusers.

Who wants to go through all that hurt and struggle to be ordinary? Remember, we all spell *struggle* the same way, but we don't all respond to it the same. Let's choose to learn from the struggle, to help the struggling, to struggle together for a better walk for all of us. We may even have to embrace the struggle. We are in the process of shedding this suit, and it hurts. Who can tell where the suit ends and the skin begins? But it's like the metamorphosis cycle. Nobody wants to go through that; however, on the other side emerges a beautiful butterfly.

Now that I know my purpose, I know that I was born to be redeemed; I can work through the metamorphosis process in this life to become a beautiful butterfly who will fly on into the next. Living from pillar to post, moving countless times, undergoing sexual abuse at the hands of men, women, friends, family members, and bosses, experiencing depression, abandonment, the gnawing in my stomach telling me I wasn't good enough for my father, for my boyfriend, for anybody—it was all worth it. The walk was worth it.

My early life was the gestational period for my true birth. That is why the walk was worth it; I was being formed for an extra-long time, under extreme duress in the birthing process, so Christ could appear to me. I look forward to the day we can walk by the sea, and I can tell Him, "Thank You for choosing me." I want to hear Him tell me the stories of the people who came before us, whose lives were changed so they could change others—so they could change mine. I want to hear the stories of all my surrogates and all their predecessors, and all the people who had to come together to change my life. I want to have Him tell me how I inspired others to change their lives and to change the world. Finally, I just want to hold His hand, and listen to Him tell me stories of when I was walking, and how He was walking right there with me.

Walking On

"Teach us to number our days."–Psalm 90:12

For my forty-first birthday, I had a vision board party to envision the next forty-one years. I had a few girlfriends over, but precariously and potently, I had my Momma. In the past I had all these questions about our relationship, about my worthiness, about her apprehension, but now the direction is clear. Walk it out with her. I wonder if Momma ever had dreams about trees. Is this leg of her life part of her redemption too? I am extremely grateful to be able to share this time with my mother. She was there when I was born, and now she is standing alongside me as I look into the future. Vision requires forgiveness and reconciliation. Momma and I are going to walk out some of these upcoming years together.

My relationship with my father is still strained. I hope and pray that someday we will have an open relationship. Until that time, I can keep making the effort, keep having high expectations, and keep believing in the possibilities. For now, he lives in L.A. and I live in Nashville, and we rarely speak. But who knows what the future will hold? I believe in the possibilities, and I believe that we are both being prepared to support each other.

David is further solidifying his relationship with his son. He already has a great relationship with his son, but we both agreed that he needs to prioritize that relationship for the next few years before his son steps into adulthood. David is also pursuing his entrepreneurial dream of owning and operating his own moving company. We are continuing to learn to love each other through our brokenness.

Jessica is still working overseas as a contractor, currently in Iraq, and she visits a frequently as she can. Just recently, within the past few months, she came to visit and spent time with my mother and me. Watching her interact with my mother brought joy to my heart. Jessica's voice is being heard.

Robert and Michael and I met by coincidence recently. We all apologized and discussed how deeply we miss one another. Our relationship issues are not totally resolved, yet we know that our love for one another is deep, and I believe in the possibilities.

Lia still lives in Nashville, and she is dealing with the loss of her son. Most of her time is spent focusing on her relationship with her younger son. She also works in a public school in Nashville, and she works with students who have special needs. We talk often.

Pam now lives in Texas, and Kim is a nurse in L.A. We all talk often and attend major events in one another's lives.

My siblings, Connie Jr., Iesheia, and Otis Jr. are all well. I look forward to creating many new memories and to our possibilities in the future.

No Name still has a place in my heart, but I have released him from all expectations. He still lives and works in L.A.

I am deeply grateful for all the opportunities I have been given, both in the past, and now in the present. My story is a simple one, one of a girl who lost her voice, and when she found it again, she used it to tell others good news—you are going *through* it.

Acknowledgments

Papa (God): Your grace is more than sufficient. You have preserved me and allowed me to endure—at the same time You protected me from myself. Thank You for choosing me for this journey.

David (Babyluv): Thank you for showing me love.

Momma: Thank you for allowing me to share my truth.

Daddy: I am looking forward to a renewed relationship with you. Until then, I love you.

Connie, Iesheia, Otis & Jazz (my siblings): I am eager to create new memories with you.

No Name: It is well with my soul.

Shameka & Aisha: The three of us were/ are inseparable. Thank you both for choosing to be my friend.

Kim & Pam: The both of you were/are so instrumental in my life. The kindness and love you gave me changed me. Because of your obedience, I am living my dream.

Lia: You are like no other. You are very special to me.

Robert & Michael: Thank you for covering me.

Jessica: God is intentional. I need you just as much as you needed me.

Ms. Parrish: Shut up! Thank you for seeking to understand and never judging me.

Dale: You are a godsend! Thank you for helping me share my truth.

Throughout this journey, I have met so many people who have impacted my life. Thank you for listening, believing, challenging, supporting, and loving *all* of me. I am forever grateful.

WORKS CITED

Atticuspoetry. "She Wore a Thousand Faces." *Instagram*, 18 Dec. 2016, www.instagram.com/p/BOK2JwLA6wj/?hl=en

Atticuspoetry. "She Conquered Her Demons." *Instagram*, 26 Jun. 2016, www.instagram.com/p/BHI0ri-hZ6M/?hl=en

Deibler, Jeromy. "Lord Move, Or Move Me." *Found a Place*, PROVIDENT, 2000, track 4. www.azlyrics.com/lyrics/ffh/lordmoveormoveme.html

Gray, S.L. "I Have Late Night Conversations with the Moon, He Tells Me about the Sun, and I Tell Him about You. S. L. Gray | Quotesies | Pinterest | Late Nights, Conversation and Moon." *Pinterest*, 2016, www.pinterest.com/pin/214554369727816520/.

Picoult, Jodi. *Salem Falls*. Pocket Books, 2014.

Cynthiatingo, "Next Life:" *Instagram*, 28 Sep. 2016.

The Holy Bible, English Standard Version. ESV® Text Edition: 2016. BibleGateway.com. www.biblegateway.com/versions/English-Standard-Version-ESV-Bible/#booklist

CPSIA information can be obtained
at www.ICGtesting.com
Printed in the USA
BVHW031018290719
554567BV00009B/307/P

9 780578 447629